DETECTIVE JARDINE

DETECTIVE JARDINE

CRIMES IN HONOLULU

by John Jardine
with Edward Rohrbough

edited by Bob Krauss

A Kolowalu Book
UNIVERSITY OF HAWAII PRESS
HONOLULU

© 1984 University of Hawaii Press
All Rights Reserved
Manufactured in the United States of America

Library of Congress Cataloging in Publication Data

Jardine, John, 1902–1969.
  Detective Jardine.

  (A Kolowalu book)
  1. Jardine, John, 1902–1969. 2. Police—Hawaii—
Honolulu—Biography. 3. Police—Hawaii—Honolulu—
History. 4. Crime and criminals—Hawaii—Honolulu—
Case studies. 5. Criminal investigation—Hawaii—
Honolulu—Case studies. I. Rohrbough, Edward, 1911–
1982. II. Krauss, Bob. III. Title. IV. Title: Crimes
in Honolulu.
HV7911.J37A33 1984   363.2'092'4 [B]   84-8671
ISBN 0-8248-0962-9

Contents

PART 2

Photo section begins on page 163.

Foreword

THE citizens of Oahu have long regarded their police force with pride, and with immense justification because the Honolulu Police Department has long been held in the highest esteem and accorded the deepest respect by its counterparts throughout the nation, if not the world. But it is not the institution that has brought about the acclaim; it is the individual men and women who have worn the badge and sworn to uphold the law to protect the well-being of all who live and visit here.

In this volume, Bob Krauss, who in earlier works has captured and embraced the concept of *aloha* in Hawaii, uses the straightforward language of Police Detective John Jardine to chronicle how a cop performs, how he separates fact from fiction, how he sets in motion the wheels of the judicial system to achieve justice. What emerges through Krauss' blue penciling of the words of the real Jardine is a police officer, intent on enforcing the law while extending infinite compassion to the violated and the violator.

There is an added dimension to the detective's memoirs: an intimate look at the sociological fabric that was distinctively Honolulu's from the 1920s to the 1950s.

It is fortunate that talk story sessions with Jardine triggered Ed Rohrbough's journalist's instinct which resulted in a productive collaboration between the two, for without Rohrbough's prodding, the main character might not have preserved the anecdotes and vivid details of criminal investigation, the essence of this literary contribution.

This book is indeed a tribute to the narrator, but it is also a solid recognition that, in spite of the human problems it had within its ranks, the Honolulu Police Department prevails as the vanguard of our personal security and safety because of officers like John Jardine.

ELEEN R. ANDERSON, *Mayor*
City and County of Honolulu

Preface

THE name John Jardine evokes in the minds of Honolulu *kama-aina*s the image of a local supersleuth: a dogged, determined, relentless detective who turned insignificant details into major clues; a ruthless hunter who never left the scent until he captured his quarry. This was an image he deliberately fostered. Another dimension of Jardine's character is less well known—a gentleness and human decency at odds with the cynical world of crime to which he was constantly exposed.

I knew little of this, however, when his widow, Roseline, asked me to edit his memoirs. So I approached the manuscript with hardly more background than most readers of this book. Only one of the crimes he investigated, the Massie case, is well known today. Screaming headlines that announced the murder by a cold-blooded maniac of Police Sergeant Henry Chillingworth, the discovery on Punahou School campus of the body of a strangled soldier, and revelations of police graft that rocked the islands have long since been buried in the files under more current sensations.

Perhaps it was my own memory of Jardine that tempted me to look at the manuscript. As a young newspaper reporter for *The Honolulu Advertiser* in the early 1950s, I knew him only by reputation. I frequently saw him standing on a downtown street corner. He always wore a rumpled, double-breasted suit and a wide-brimmed, George Raft hat pulled down over his hawklike face. He stood silently watching people go by as if checking their faces in his mental card file. To me he *looked* like a detective.

The manuscript soon stirred my interest for another reason. It is absolutely realistic. Jardine makes no attempt to gloss over the sordidness of the crimes he investigated. He dealt with hoodlums, thieves, con men, killers, pimps, stool pigeons, gamblers, and prostitutes who peopled a level of society of Honolulu that has never been written about in our history books. He describes Hell's Half Acre, Mosquito Flats, Blood Alley, the Chancre Barn, and Honolulu Rooms with attention usually reserved for Iolani Palace and the Royal Hawaiian Hotel.

The book is a human document revealing a dimension of the past that too often remains untold in narratives that stress the "big picture." Jardine tells how it feels for a veteran cop who owns neither a house nor a car to be offered a bribe of $75,000. He wrings the confession of murder from a young man who is the son of an acquaintance. After catching a killer who has remained free for twenty-two years, he lets her go home overnight before arresting her so that she can make peace with God and her family. He becomes pallbearer for a fellow police officer who confessed in disgrace to wholesale involvement in graft which Jardine himself uncovered.

For practical purposes, this book serves as a history of the Honolulu Police Department from 1923, when Jardine became a rookie cop on the tough Aala Park beat, to the 1950s, when he breaks off his narrative. During this period, his fellow officers were as colorful as the criminals they pursued. They included the legendary Chang Apana, the model for fictional detective Charlie Chan; ebullient and controversial Police Chief William Gabrielson who resigned during the police graft investigation; and veteran Officer Holburn Akiona who taught Jardine as a rookie how to sober up a drunk, use his feet in a fight, and where to sleep in an alley without getting caught on night watch. Jardine describes reform of the Police Department in 1932 after intense criticism over its handling of the Massie case, and another major upheaval within the department as a result of the police graft investigation in 1946.

The chapters concerning the police graft scandal are of an unusual nature and therefore have been taken out of chronological sequence to form a separate part of the book, and their handling deserves special mention. Jardine's investigation with Val Cederlof of alleged gambling payoffs to police officers resulted in widespread criticism of the Honolulu Police Department. At the same time, a great many people were gambling. The popularity of this illegal activity is revealed in the following quote from *The Honolulu Advertiser* of Saturday, April 13, 1946:

> Although the places involved in the present police scandal are located in Chinatown, there are said to be other places operating in the residential areas and in certain hotels of the city. The Chinatown area is considered the most lucrative.
>
> Games operating in these places include "craps," poker, Chinese fan-tan (played with beans) and in some places other forms of Oriental gambling. Fan-tan is reported to be among the most popular games because of the speed with which money may change hands. One place specializes in dice games.
>
> Stories of local businessmen losing large sums of money and of plantation laborers leaving with comfortable fortunes after a few hours are reported common in certain circles. As an example, the owner of a large downtown market is said to have lost $10,000 playing fan-tan while another business is reported to have sunk $40,000 in another game of fan-tan. In some games, a player has to have at least $1,000 to "get in" while other games are operated on a more modest scale for the benefit of the little fellow.
>
> Local gamblers, of course, favor the legalization of gambling in Hawaii but have little hope that the legislature will ever take such action. Legalization, they argue, would do away with the need for "paying protection."
>
> In the meantime, organized vice is waiting for the present investigation to "cool off" before making new plans in the interests of maintaining a very profitable industry.

Gambling was conducted in private homes and in the back rooms of filling stations. A former gambler informed me that he played in games at Waikiki hotels, the Waialae Country Club, and in the locker room at Palama Settlement where crap games were broken up by the settlement director. Witnesses in court testified that two hundred fifty to three hundred people patronized one Chinatown gambling house daily. Honolulu at the time obviously had a high tolerance for this illegal activity. In such a climate, policemen were put in a difficult position. Stamping out such a broadly approved crime must have been like plugging a sieve.

Greedy policemen found it safe and easy to collect bribes. Honest policemen found it difficult to defend themselves against charges of bribery by gamblers angry about being arrested, especially if they had paid a member of the force for protection.

Newspaper reports following the graft trials indicate that the public felt it was unjust that only one policeman was convicted when others may have shared the guilt. Friends of the convicted man, Captain Clarence Caminos, signed a petition asking for his pardon on the grounds that "his conviction of bribery arose out of an unusual set of circumstances whereby he was singled out to pay the penalty for certain practices which were widely prevalent in the Honolulu Police Department at the time."

Later, the Territorial Board of Pardons recommended to the governor that the sentence be reduced to three months, partly on the grounds that singling this officer out for punishment from the twenty-six indicted amounted to "a travesty of justice." This started a drawn-out controversy among newspaper readers, editors, and attorneys. Attorney General C. Nils Tavares, later a federal judge, argued that in his opinion failure to convict other policemen was due to the granting of immunity to the one most guilty so that he would agree to testify. The editor of *The Honolulu Advertiser* wrote that the miscarriage of justice, if any, lay not in the conviction of a guilty man but in freeing others who may have been guilty.

Jardine was put in a position more difficult than that of the Vice Squad, investigating charges of bribery brought mostly by gamblers against fellow police officers. Jardine's investigation shed light on this little known period of history in Honolulu, but it also inadvertently involved policemen who were later acquitted of bribe-taking and who went on to lead productive and honorable lives.

I assume that it was for this reason, to protect the innocent, Jardine and Rohrbough used fictitious names for the policemen under investigation. I have, therefore, followed their lead. The only policemen named are the captain who was convicted and the sergeant who confessed. In fairness, I have dealt with the identities of alleged gamblers in the same way, providing the names of only those persons who testified to illegal activities under oath in court. In another chapter, also, I have changed the names of a confessed murderer and her victim simply because the sequence of events is so tragic it seems a shame to identify the families.

I have made no attempt to gloss over the unsavory parts. The manuscript stands as a unique document which could have been written only by a policeman intimate with the seamy side of Honolulu in his day. I have tried to preserve the uniqueness of Jardine's style by making as few revisions as possible while editing down an overly long manuscript and adjusting the time frame so that events will make sense to present-day readers.

This book's rich vein of unusual experience might have gone undiscovered without the effort and foresight of another person who encouraged Jardine to tell his story and put it down on paper. Journalist Edward Rohrbough took down Jardine's recollections and transformed copious notes into the detective's memoirs. It was my pleasure to have a longstanding professional and personal association with Ed Rohrbough, a big man physically with a rugged exterior and a warm, kindly disposition. However, I had no idea that Ed had worked with Jardine on the manuscript until it came into my possession.

Edward Rohrbough, Jr., was born in Glenville, West Virginia, on June 6, 1911. Ed earned his bachelor of arts degree at Glenville State College and his masters at the University of Texas. He also attended the University of Virginia and the National University of Mexico. From 1940 to 1943, he worked as a reporter for the *Toronto Star* and later for *Newsweek*. In 1943, Ed joined the U.S. Office of War Information. He was assigned to the China office in Chungking in 1944. After VJ Day, Ed quit the OWI and journeyed as a freelance journalist to areas of China liberated by the New Fourth Army (Communist). His dispatches were carried by *United Press* and by the *China Weekly Review*.

In 1946, he returned to New York where he freelanced, writing fiction and articles for publications including the *New York Herald Tribune* and the *New York Daily News*. He worked for the *Honolulu Record,* published in Honolulu, and after it folded in 1958, for the brief-lived *Honolulu Reporter.* When Jack Burns became governor in 1962, Ed went into his administration and eventually became an administrative assistant. He later worked in a similar capacity for Governor George Ariyoshi before retiring in 1978. He died in 1982.

His wife, Jeanette, said he knew a lot of old-timers on the police force and that he liked to "talk story" with them. He and Jardine became friends. Jeanette said she believes their collaboration took place around 1958 or 1959, when Ed had more time on his hands. She said Jardine would write in longhand and Ed would rewrite the stories.

A number of people deserve thanks for their help in bringing this manuscript to completion. First are Roseline Jardine, widow of the author, and Jeanette Rohrbough, widow of his collaborator. Also publisher Robert Sparks who had faith in the book. Former Police Chief Dan Liu provided valuable information as did retired *Advertiser* sports editor Vernon "Red" McQueen and veteran attorney Arthur Trask. Former Public Prosecutor and retired Circuit Court Judge William Z. Fairbanks deserves special thanks for graciously reading part of the manuscript for accuracy. I am also grateful to attorney Jeffrey S. Portnoy for reading portions of the book to check legal concerns. My thanks go to the librarians of the Hawaii Newspaper Agency—especially head librarian Beatrice Kaya—for assistance in research.

I am grateful to the *Honolulu Star-Bulletin* and *The Honolulu Advertiser,* the Archives of Hawaii, and the Bishop Museum for permitting reproduction of photographs. Special mention should be made of Police Department photos donated to the Archives by former police photographer Abel Fraga. This was the primary source of photos of policemen named in this book. Finally, my warm *mahalo* to Mayor Eileen Anderson for her contribution.

BOB KRAUSS

PART 1

1

Up from Alapai

WHY did I become a policeman, a detective apprehending criminals, when so many of my friends and acquaintances became the lawbreakers against whom the work of my whole life has been directed? This is a question I have often pondered. Perhaps the answer lies somewhere in my own beginnings.

Honolulu was a rough town in 1902. I was born here on May 28 of that year in the Alapai section of the city. While not the roughest area, it was still a far cry from the silk-stocking districts of Punahou, Makiki, and Manoa where the directors of the Big Five plantation, shipping, and merchandising companies lived.

Compared to the modern city of Honolulu today, the place into which I was born was a country town. True, it was a seaport, but ships were fewer and much farther between. It had been an American port only a few years, and there were still people in the town who weren't sure they liked the idea of being American. The memory of Hawaiian royalty was almost as vivid in those days as the shadows of our tropical foliage cutting sharp patterns in the bright sunlight. Country town or not, Honolulu was still very conscious of having once been the capital of a kingdom.

Likewise, our society and our homes gave very tangible evidence of a pattern all its own. Many of the inhabitants of Honolulu had been brought to the islands to work in the sugar fields and in the fields of the new but thriving pineapple industry. There were Chinese from Canton, Japanese from the farming districts of Japan and Okinawa, Spaniards, Austrians, Koreans, Filipinos, Puerto Ricans, Russians from Harbin, and Portuguese.

On the plantations, they had been housed in camps according to their national origins. Those who moved to Honolulu had found jobs of an industrial nature or had saved their money and

3

started small businesses. They had stayed and reared families and now were settled in communities of their own. Just as there were places called Old Chinese Camp and Filipino Camp on plantations, so there were settlements of national groups in Honolulu. Even in some of the teeming urban tenement areas, the people called their housing sections camps.

But more broadly, there were whole areas of the city, known as quarters, for these national groups. On Maunakea Street in downtown Honolulu, you bought foods and herbs imported from Hong Kong. In many parts of town, but especially in Moiliili, you shopped at stores with the names announced in Japanese characters alongside the English lettering. Many Puerto Ricans lived in the Lanakila section of town, and many Portuguese in Kakaako and in the Alapai district.

My father, John Jardine, Sr., a native of Portugal, was a resident of Hawaii by another means of ingress from that of being imported to work on plantations. He had first seen the beautiful island of Oahu from the deck of a whaler on which he was serving as a seaman in 1880. As seamen have done ever since our islands became ports of call, and as they do to this day, my father decided Hawaii was the place where he wanted to spend the rest of his life. So it was natural enough that he made his "home port" a large, two-bedroom house on Alapai Street.

There was a Portuguese colony in Honolulu when he arrived and so my father felt at home. A tall, powerfully built man, he had no trouble getting a job as a coal-passer on the waterfront. Later, his skill and industry earned him a job as gardener for the Territory, a job he held until his retirement in 1918.

My mother did not arrive from Portugal until some years later, after my father had established himself. The couple were married in Hawaii, and in their house on Alapai, they set up a household and family typical of the local Portuguese community of that day. Beginning with my two brothers and three sisters, there were always plenty of people around our house, especially on weekends.

Saturday mornings I would go to where my father worked and help him with chores that would wind up his work for the week. Then we'd go down to the Kekaulike Fish Market, stopping on the way to buy five gallons of wine. At the fish market my father would usually meet old friends—sometimes Mayor Joe Fern. Father would address the mayor in Portuguese and the mayor, though Hawaiian, would answer in broken Portuguese of his own. Mayor Fern would also speak phrases of Chinese, Japanese, and other languages to friends of other national backgrounds. The fish market was to Mayor Fern, my father, and a lot of other old-timers what the country store was to many a rural town on the mainland.

For fifteen cents, my father would buy a fish a yard long and we'd go back uptown, Father a fine strapping figure of a man with his height and his black handlebar mustache, which was the fashion of the day. This time our destination would be Dick Sullivan's Two Jacks Saloon. I would wait outside with the fish and wine while my father had a few shots of whiskey and "talked stories" with his pals. Then he'd come out, steady as ever, and we'd go home to portion out the wine in smaller jugs while the women cut up the fish and prepared it for cooking.

On Saturday nights, Portuguese musicians would drop around with their twelve-string guitars, mandolins, and instruments we called "taro patch," which were, I believe, the forerunners of the ukulele, now known as a Hawaiian instrument.* They were fine musicians and they had large repertoires of Portuguese songs; so there would be singing and dancing until late at night. Our friends would drop in to play cards and drink, and the evening would be one long, noisy, happy event. On Sunday morning we'd all get up for early mass, then come home and start the music and drinking all over again. On Monday everybody would be back hard at work, just waiting, no doubt, for another weekend of fun and frolic.

Our section was not, perhaps, as notorious for gang fights and hoodlumism as were some other parts of town, such as Palama, Kalihi, and Kakaako. What made it rough were the many visits we had from boys and young men from those notorious districts. But I remember two brothers in our own neighborhood who fought with

*The "taro patch," a descendant of the Portuguese *rajao*, was a five-stringed instrument somewhat larger than a ukulele but smaller than a guitar. *The Honolulu Advertiser*, October 13, 1975.

the cops every time they drank heavily—which was whenever they got the money or had the drinks set up. They were fierce street brawlers who could take care of most assailants, and they gave the police many a stiff workout. But alcohol and beatings from police clubs finally landed them both in the Territorial Hospital for the insane at Kaneohe.

Then there was another young fellow who didn't like the police —and with good reason. He was a burglar and he always carried a revolver. One afternoon the cops cornered him on the side of Punchbowl and ordered him to surrender. He decided to use the pistol instead. There was a hot exchange of fire for awhile, until he ran out of ammunition and gave up. He had apparently run out of luck, too, for he was convicted and served a long term in prison. Eventually he died there, serving another sentence.

Those were the older boys in my community, but many of my own contemporaries had similar tendencies. Three of my friends worked out a stunt to make spending money that would have landed them in Oahu Prison* if they had been caught. They would climb atop the buildings of downtown business establishments in broad daylight and go to work tearing out the lead along the eaves and roof joints as if they were hired for the job. They'd throw the lead down in strips and chunks and haul it away to the junkyard to sell.

It was the type of theft few building owners suspected, and often the crime wouldn't come to anyone's attention until the next rain when the water came down through the uncovered spots in rivulets and showers. In fact, the mother of one of this trio gave them the narrowest escape they had. She happened to pass along a street one day and she looked up to see her son, who had no great reputation for industry, energetically laboring up on a rooftop with a companion.

"Jimmy!" yelled the startled woman. "What are you doing up there?"

Even more startled, Jimmy yelled back, "Go home! Go home now and don't hang around! I'll tell you later."

*What is now known as Oahu Community Correctional Center was called Oahu Prison before Hawaii became a state.

Needless to say, what he told her later was at some variance with the truth.

The cops in those days were mostly Hawaiians, and we seldom lost an opportunity to heckle them with such cries as "There go the Honolulu poi dogs!" When they passed our way, we often accompanied the shouts with a barrage of clods and stones that would dent the wire mesh sides of the horse-drawn patrol wagon. They chased us but seldom caught any of us. If they had caught me, I think I would have feared punishment at the hands of my father more than anything they might have done. I was certainly in so much mischief with the other boys that, looking back, I wonder how I was lucky enough to avoid ever getting picked up by the police—and instead eventually becoming one of them.

Some of the police of that day were mounted and armed with long blacksnake whips. Generally we paid these more respect. They could reach out with their long lashes and lasso a fugitive who might think he was in the clear. Occasionally one would ride a boy down under the hooves of his mount. Among these was Chang Apana, who later graduated to the police Detective Division and who became the model for the fictional Charlie Chan.

One of these old-time cops to whom we gave an unusually bad time was called Fly Lid. He had the job of patrolling around the Territorial Normal School where I was enrolled early. Often when there were school dances, some of us would gather on the fire escape outside to watch. The cop would see us from down below and shout at us to get down.

We'd yell, "Go on home, Fly Lid!" As often as not, we'd dump a waste basket full of trash on his head. He'd chase us and we'd go through the school and outrun him.

Like the youth of today, we ran together in groups that had some characteristics of gangs. And because of the racial setup of the various parts of town, more often than not we'd pull our mischief on some other racial group. The Japanese, for instance, always left their shoes outside on the porch. So we'd go to a house where they were having a big dinner or a game or some kind of party, and while they drank *sake* inside we'd work on the shoes out on the porch, tying all the shoelaces together. Then we'd throw a bunch of shoes in through the door and holler, *"Banzai!"* and take off. They never caught us.

The Chinese got it even worse from us. With their long braided queues they were natural targets for our youthful, unthinking rowdyism. In 1911 Dr. Sun Yat-sen headed the revolution to throw out the Manchurian warlords and at the same time to modernize China. He had many ideas as to how this feat should be accomplished. One of them was to eliminate queues, which he claimed were unsanitary and relics of feudalism. It became a patriotic act in China to cut off one's queue. Millions of them disappeared and gave place to more modern haircuts.

But here in Honolulu we had many diehards among the Chinese old-timers. They kept on wearing their hair in queues for many years after the revolution in China, some letting them hang down their backs, some wearing them coiled on top of their heads. Many of the queue-wearing Chinese operated poi factories, worked rice paddies, and peddled fruits and vegetables from pushcarts. These peddlers were natural prey for mischievous boys.

We liked the fruit but seldom felt like paying for it. Of course the pushcart peddler didn't like our pilfering, but his queue put him at our mercy, for when he came after us he was likely to be swung by his queue with a shout of "Ho John!" While he worried about his hair, the thieves would make their escape, each with an armload of fruit.

Nor did this rough stuff need the inspiration of fruit. Sometimes when we were making the rounds of the town we'd come up on a Chinese from behind. One of us would grab his queue and yank, bringing him to his haunches. We might drag him a few feet while he screamed bloody murder before the one holding the queue would let go, and we'd all take off laughing at the poor fellow's screams of outrage.

But you could push the Chinese, or any of the other groups, too far. One night a member of our gang decided merely pulling queues was too tame. He sneaked up behind a lean Chinese and cut off about ten inches of his queue with a pair of scissors. The Chinese yelled as if he'd been stuck with a knife and ran to the hand laundry where he worked. That night seven Chinese from

8

the laundry, including the fellow who had lost part of his queue, went on the prowl to try to find the pranksters who had been harassing them.

So one of our gang tried a new tactic. He called the police to tell them a group of Chinese armed with knives was out on the town and ready to commit murder. The police intercepted the Chinese not far from our district, at the corner of Punchbowl and Miller streets, and lined them up against a fence for a search. The members of our gang were hiding in some bushes across the street watching the whole show. It turned out to be both farcical and pathetic.

The Chinese could speak almost no English. They protested loudly, making gestures toward the one who had his queue trimmed. The cops understood nothing of what they said, of course, and talked Hawaiian among themselves, paying no attention to the oratory of the Chinese, keeping them lined up against the fence all the while.

In the search, the police found all the Chinese had knives except the one whose queue had been cut off. He had a cleaver. When he saw the search was inevitable, he pulled the cleaver from the waistband of his baggy cotton pants and stuck it into the fence with a thud that sounded only too clearly over in our clump of bushes. When they finished the search, the police threw the Chinese into the patrol wagon and hauled them down to the station. I never heard how they were charged or what happened to them.

Our queue-pulling ended when the Chinese protests brought some effective police action. One of the old-time detectives disguised himself as a Chinese peddler and pushed his wares in a cart until some hoodlum fell into the trap and pulled the wrong queue. The law of old Hawaii thus intervened and protected local Chinese against the edict of Dr. Sun—at least when the edict was being enforced by young hoodlums like me and my wild friends.

During my eighth-grade year at the Normal School, I happened upon a scene that probably had the most to do with the turn of my own career toward the law instead of against it. One day at noon when I came home for lunch, I found a gang of men with picks and shovels digging a trench in front of our house. All were dressed in striped suits, some red and white, some blue and white. Some of the men wore chains around their ankles to which were attached iron balls. When they moved from place to place along the trench, they picked up the iron balls and carried them to make movement easier. On the other side of the street stood a guard with a rifle cradled in his arm, watching their every move.

I was shocked. I had never seen men dressed like this working under guard, though I had heard enough to know they must be convicts—murderers, burglars, and thieves doing sentences at Oahu Prison. I have never forgotten the details of that scene. Nor have I forgotten what it meant to me then. I resolved firmly that I would never spend any part of my life wearing one of those striped suits. No matter how tough life might get, I decided then and there, it couldn't get worse than it was for the unfortunate men in that gang who carried the stigma of the convict along with their slavelike punishment. So, you see, I might have wound up wearing a striped suit as a number in Oahu Prison instead of wearing a badge as a member of the Honolulu police force if the convicts had not been assigned to work in front of our house that day.

In 1918 the lure of high wages paid workers during World War I ended my formal education. I was a young buck and, like all boys who grow up in the islands, only too anxious to see the wonders of the mainland, U.S.A. So at sixteen I decided I was a man, took off for Seattle and before long was working in a lumberyard at Cosmopolis, Washington. A year on that job was enough. I returned to Seattle and went from there to San Francisco, arriving the day Jack Dempsey whipped Jess Willard for the heavyweight championship, July 4, 1919. It was also the day the state of California went dry.

After two years working as a chauffeur and in garages, I decided I'd had enough and shipped out for Honolulu, working as an oiler in the engine room of a freighter. Nothing distinguished the voyage for me except that I met a seaman named John R. Troche and we became friends. In the years to come, John Troche, who was also destined to become a cop, was to figure in many of my most important cases.

I knocked around at several jobs for the next two years, working my longest hitch for three months at the City and County Electric Light Department. Then in November 1922 I went to work for the city's Water and Sewer Works Department and stayed there until I decided to try out for the police force.

Probably the credit, or blame, for that decision should go to Manuel Santos, who became better known to the whole population of Honolulu by his nickname, Hapai Mountain (that is, "Can Lift a Mountain"). He had come by his name in the way workers on plantations get such names, because he was a strong man. He established a reputation in later years as a "character" in Honolulu, to be hailed and loved by the people for his humorous antics and impromptu theatricals at athletic events.

When we worked together at the Water and Sewer Works Department, it was Hapai Mountain who had the ambition to be a cop, not me. He showed me a clipping from the newspaper that told how Sheriff Charles H. Rose was looking for men and urged me to go to the station with him for a tryout. I was reluctant, but Santos insisted and finally I agreed. There, we filled out formal applications.

Not long afterward, we found ourselves among a crowd of husky young men, many of them stevedores from the waterfront a block away, reporting at Pete Baron's gym for Police Department physical examinations. The competition looked plenty strong. Pete Baron was an old-time athlete and gymnast. He was out to let us know from the beginning that we were choosing a career that would be no bed of roses. He called the roll and began, "So you fellows want to be cops, eh? Well, we'll soon see how good you are."

First we went through chinning tests on horizontal bars and wall bars. There were squats, push-ups, and sit-ups. Then we did ten laps around the gym, hurdling a three-foot tape each time. Next was weight lifting. We hoisted dumbbells that weighed twenty-five, fifty, and one hundred pounds. Before Pete was through with us, he had us hanging on the ropes. We privately bet with one another that half the cops on the force couldn't pass the tests we'd been through.

The gymnast scored each of our tests. After a few days, Santos and I were informed we had passed. Next we had the written test to be taken at McKinley High School. When we reported for that one, we found the crowd considerably smaller. Plenty of the long-shoremen hadn't been as athletic as they looked.

At that time the educational requirement was only that the applicant have an eighth-grade education, so many of the questions and problems were simple. In spelling, geography, and history, however, the test was somewhat specialized. Hawaii was already conscious of becoming a tourist mecca and the questions reflected it. As policemen we would be required to give directions to tourists and to visitors from the outer islands of Hawaii, Maui, Kauai, and Molokai. So we were expected not only to be able to spell Kamehameha, Kawaiahao, Iolani, Kaiulani, and the like, but also to know what those names signified and what points of interest they were attached to. To be really complete, our answers would sound as if they had come from a tourist guidebook.

There was more reason for testing this sort of thing than you might think. For one thing, a few of the older policemen were Hawaiians who spoke limited English, though they were fluent in Hawaiian, and they had trouble understanding tourists from the mainland and even more trouble making themselves understood. In one notable case, a big Hawaiian cop stopped an automobile in downtown Honolulu at night and warned the driver, "You *kukui* no *'a'ā*." The driver, a tourist, was completely bewildered, though any resident of the islands at that time would have known the policeman was saying, "Your taillight has gone out."

Confusion about points of interest was just as bad. There was the tourist who stopped a policeman and asked, "Can you tell me the way to the aquarium?"

The cop looked bewildered and asked, "The what?"

"The aquarium," the tourist repeated. "You know, where they keep fish."

The cop's face lit up. "Oh, fish. Sure, you go that way." He gave perfect directions that landed the tourist square in front of the teeming, noisy, smelly Kekaulike Fish Market.

All of us knew the story, and so we weren't surprised that *aquarium* was one of the words on our spelling test.

A couple of weeks later, Hapai Mountain and I got letters from the Civil Service Commission informing us we had passed all the tests. Then, after a few days, we received letters from Sheriff Rose telling us to be at his office at 9 A.M., July 16, 1923. We learned by word of mouth that the grading had been based largely on our physical strength and agility: Pete Baron's examination counted for sixty percent, the written exam for forty percent. In those days the emphasis in police work was still on strong backs rather than on the officer's mental ability.

We had won our way onto the police force and Hapai Mountain was happy. Frankly, I didn't know whether to shout or cry. I thought, well, it would be something new. If I didn't like it I could quit. It took me a lot of years to discover that even though you may not always like what you're doing, there are other considerations to keep you on the job.

2

Tricks of a New Trade

IN the night shadows at the edge of Aala Park, two men were engaged in a pantomime as strange to me as the movements of a Chinese opera. One was inert, prone on the grass in the park. The other held him by the heels and swung his legs back and forth in vigorous half-circles. The act was familiar to Officer Holburn Akiona, a veteran cop, who stood by me and who had first noticed the movement. He silently brought me to a halt.

"He's doing a couple of things," said Akiona in whispers. "First, he's testing the drunk to see if he's passed out enough to roll. If the drunk gets up, there'll be a chase. If he stays passed out, he'll get rolled. But if he gets up and fights the guy off, this punk will come back to look for the change he may have shaken out of the drunk's pockets."

Akiona had taken off his cap with the glittering badge and he held his arm so as to cover the bright buttons of his uniform. I did the same. Now, as we watched, the lush-artist dropped the prone man's heels, looked this way and that to see if anyone was looking, and failing to spot us, went quickly through the drunk's pockets. He pulled out an object which he transferred to his own pocket, straightened up, and began to walk swiftly away.

"Come on," grunted Akiona, and we were after him.

We collared him at the corner of King and Aala streets, within a hundred feet of where the drunk lay. I searched him and in a moment found a man's wallet with $76 in it. Our prisoner was an islander of mixed origin. He responded to Akiona's brisk questioning nervously. Looking in the wallet, I found a name different from the name he gave. Akiona pressed that point and asked him where he got the wallet. At first he claimed he had found it in the park rest room that afternoon. A few more sharp questions had him confessing he had stolen it from the drunk. We walked him back to where the drunk lay on the grass, still snoozing peacefully.

Akiona shook the drunk but the man slept on. He then lifted one of the man's feet by the toe of his shoe and gave him a light crack on the insole with his club. Still the drunk didn't move.

"Sometimes we have to take the treatment a little farther," said Akiona philosophically.

As I stood watch over the prisoner, Akiona knelt down to lift the drunk's head in his hands, his palms behind the man's ears. Then he rubbed back and forth rapidly, at the same time lifting the man to his feet. When the drunk was upright, Akiona thrust him off. The drunk staggered backward and sat down, then got up again, if not sobered, at least half-conscious.

We questioned him. He identified the driver's license in the wallet and said he had about $75 in it. Akiona told him to see the captain of detectives at the police station to reclaim his property the next morning, then sent him home in a cab and warned him to sober up if he didn't want to go to jail himself. We then took our prisoner to the nearest police box to call the patrol wagon.

It was my first pinch, and even though I was participating only in the secondary role of a rookie, it turned out to be a good one. At the station, the thief confessed to twenty-five house burglaries and robberies. Technically, I had been on the police force for a week, but I had discovered enough of the new world I'd entered to know it would be a long time before I'd be anything like a good cop. There were a lot of things to learn, and although I was working hard at it, I could see it was going to take time.

My new world had begun at the appointed hour on July 16 with an appearance at the office of the chief police clerk, Clement K. Wong who, I soon discovered, was known behind his back as the Shrinking Violet. I was to learn that Clem was the majordomo of the police station, the real, titled custodian of the building. If you wanted to see the sheriff in a hurry, you had to talk to Clem. If you had a friend in trouble, Clem would be the best bet for help or suggestions. If you had anything to sell the Police Department, Clem was the man you had to convince, and he guarded the purse

15

strings of the taxpayer like the staunchest sort of watchdog. Clem wouldn't give a pencil to the sheriff himself until he got proof there was no lead in the old pencil.

But all that I was to learn later. That morning Clem Wong was a big man in the eyes of Hapai Mountain Santos and me because he took us in to introduce us to even bigger men, Sheriff Charles Rose and his deputy, Julius Ash. In short order we were sworn in, given our police commissions signed by the sheriff, and led to the property room by Clem Wong. Wong gave us our cap shields and belts with the word *Police* on the buckles, our clubs and silver-plated buttons. Then he told us to have our uniforms made. Each policeman was required to pay for his own uniform and his gun.

Santos and I went next to the recommended tailor. Each of us ordered a blue serge uniform with coat and pants, and two extra pairs of white cotton trousers. In those days the foot patrol officers on the day watch dressed in blue caps, blue coats, and white pants, with the belt looped around the coat, and they carried a holder for the club. On the afternoon and night watches, we wore blues altogether, hence the need for blue pants, which were not quite so conspicuous after the sun went down. Not very long before I joined the force, patrol officers had worn helmets fashioned after those used by the English bobbies. But these had been eliminated.

Likewise, the Honolulu "mounties," a sort of elite among the uniformed cops, were gone. They had worn khaki uniforms and campaign hats, ridden horses, and carried the long blacksnake whips I referred to earlier—and which gave them respect in the rough areas of town. We were not to get a crack at this assignment, for the motorcycle had replaced the horse at the same time the helmets disappeared. To the old-timers, the mechanization of the police was just as unpleasant as the mechanization of the U.S. Army was to prove to the old cavalrymen later. When the change took place in 1923, most of the mounties transferred to bikes and the rest went to substations in the outlying districts.

Santos drew the day watch and went on duty at once. I was assigned to the afternoon watch and told to come back at 2:15 P.M. for duty. It was about 11 A.M. when I left the police station. I don't mind saying I was all a jumble of emotions. I had a very light lunch and went to Emma Square, then one of the main centers of the city, and sat down on a bench to ponder my future.

What kind of a law enforcement officer would I be? Suddenly I had put myself in a position where I would have to change viewpoints. No longer could I sympathize with young men who yelled "Honolulu poi dogs!" at the cops and threw clods and rocks at the patrol wagons. I would *be* one of the "poi dogs." Now it would be my duty to pursue and arrest young men who stole the lead off roofs to sell for their own profit, and young men who harassed Chinese immigrant workers by pulling and cutting off their queues.

At the same time, I would be up against the most dangerous men the islands could produce or attract: street brawlers, maniacs, murderers, thieves, fleecers, pimps, and burglars. I had thought about it all before, of course, but that noon period seemed like a zero hour. I still hadn't actually gone on duty. Somewhere in the back of my mind I must have felt there was still time to get out. In the end, I decided I would try to be a "good cop." I resolved I would try to do my duty honestly without unnecessarily pushing anyone around. To this day, I can't think of anything more that can be expected of a police officer.

With plenty of time to spare, I wandered down to the battered old station house on Merchant Street and climbed the sagging stairs to the patrol room where I reported to Captain Walter Fieldgrove. His sergeant, Abel Kauhaihao, and the men of the afternoon watch were getting into their uniforms. As I watched them dress, I noticed their clubs were different from the one Clem Wong had given me. These clubs were longer and had holes in the handles through which leather thongs could be fitted.

Before I could ask any questions, the captain brought us to attention. First he called me forward, introduced me to the other men, and told me to take my place in line. He addressed the Fort Street beat officer, George Kelai, and told him I was being assigned to him for the day. Each succeeding day, the captain said, I would be assigned to a different beat officer until I had acquainted myself with the beats in the city.

The captain gave us a short résumé of what had occurred on the

17

preceding watch and dismissed us to disperse to our beats. On the way to Fort Street, I asked George Kelai about the long clubs with holes in the handles. He explained that the club I had was a regulation police club made of *kiawe* wood, which was not very hard to split. Most officers had their own clubs made to order out of lignum vitae wood, he said, because it is tough and won't split. The leather thong secured the club in the hand, a precaution that might sometime pay dividends in a hard fight. He offered to ask a friend of his, a pattern maker, to make me a club. I told him I had a friend at the Honolulu Iron Works who could do the job.

When we arrived at Fort and Queen streets, Kelai told me his beat began there and ended at Vineyard Street. The Fort Street beat ran from the waterfront toward the mountains in the general direction of Pacific Heights, a fairly wealthy residential district. Fort Street was a main street of the city, a street of smart shops, office buildings, large stores, occasional restaurants, hotels, a theater, the Catholic cathedral, and, in its farthest reaches, homes.

On following days, I covered the downtown beats successively, which gave me a thorough working knowledge of the city at the time. It was a colorful place, full of startling contrasts. The historic governor's mansion, with its broad lawn and majestic overhanging trees, lay not far from tawdry River Street, where farmers brought their produce by day and gamblers ran their games by night. Waterfront docks merged with Chinatown shops, in which reed baskets and shelves bulged with ginger root, dried seaweed, mushrooms, shark fins, black-encrusted salt eggs, and herbs. Nearby were Tin Can Alley, Blood Town, Mosquito Flats, and Hell's Half Acre,* where whores, pimps, thugs, and footpads roamed only a few blocks from Honolulu Hale, the city hall, where the mayor and city officials had their offices. Kekaulike Street, where Hawaiian lei makers sat all day weaving beautiful wreaths of *pikake,* carnations, gardenias, plumerias, and other flowers, ran parallel to

---

*Mosquito Flats in Iwilei, noted for prostitution, was a swampy area infested with mosquitoes. Blood Town adjoined Aala Park. Tin Can Alley ran *mauka* off Beretania Street into Hell's Half Acre, a tenement area of crooked paths, sagging balconies, and rickety wood stairs. Under the Kukui Redevelopment Program, begun in 1960, high-rise condominiums have replaced the wooden tenements.

the north side of Nuuanu Street, where Japanese cooks served steaming bowls of noodles, rice, fish, pork, and vegetables.

Officer Kelai told me about police procedure. He explained that we must make a routine call every hour from the police signal box on the beat to the switchboard operator in the station house. He showed me how to make the calls, how to use the box to talk to the operator, and how to set the lever for a riot call. He also told me we'd work an eight-hour shift every day, seven days a week: 6:40 A.M. to 2:40 P.M., 2:40 P.M. to 10:40 P.M., or 10:40 P.M. to 6:40 A.M. This schedule was rotated every two weeks. When the shifts rotated, it was sixteen hours on duty and eight hours off. Every sixth week, Kelai said, we would have a day off. I figured I would be able to use it.

That first afternoon-night hitch on Fort Street was peaceful enough. I felt thankful that the captain had decided to start me out easy. The next day I went to the Honolulu Iron Works to see my friend Alfred Joseph, a pattern maker, who told me he'd be glad to make a lignum vitae club for me without charge.

At the end of my tour of the police beats of the city, I was assigned to accompany Officer Holburn Akiona on the King Street beat, and there my baptism of action came, as I have told, with the pinch of a thief rolling a drunk. Akiona, my first real teacher in police work, was well fitted for the job, and of this I was glad because Aala Park was on the beat, which made it one of the toughest in town. Aala Park was a central gathering place for the working people of Honolulu for years. Situated in the middle of slum housing, the park was always the scene of much thievery and violence.

Akiona, a tall rugged man, standing over six feet and weighing about one hundred eighty-five pounds, had had plenty of experience. But he had a gentler side, too, for he would never carry a pistol, a pattern I had observed. Following his example, I never carried a pistol except when some superior caught me without one and ordered me to put it on. I didn't want to kill anyone and I still don't. In those days, the wearing of pistols wasn't yet compulsory.

Our first pinch was the beginning of a night of action not much unlike any other night on the beat. Aala Park abounded with hip-

19

pocket bootleggers, the drunks that resulted from them, and the rollers that in turn followed the drunks. Farther on was a taxi-dance place known far and wide as Chancre Barn, which featured whores and pimps as well as the sellers of stimulants. On the same beat was Hell's Half Acre, which ran from Blood Town and Mosquito Flats to Tin Can Alley, and comprised a sort of no-man's-land, most of which was off limits to servicemen. Strangers stayed away from Hell's Half Acre in those days. A man could get himself slugged or knifed any night there, just by being present. A thug could dodge in and out of a maze of alleyways and narrow lanes, making pursuit almost impossible.

Akiona guided me about the beat, pointing out this bootlegger, that pimp, the other ex-con just out of Oahu Prison. I could see we had plenty of potential customers. He also expounded on various ways of rousing drunks, some of which sounded a little rough. If a rap on the sole and a vigorous rubbing of the ears didn't work, there were other methods to try. You might put your fingernail under the drunk's, he said, and press on the nerve. He advised against this, however, because the subject would feel the results long after he'd forgotten the hangover from his drunk. A cigaret paper version of the hotfoot was another method. You wet one end of a cigaret paper, stick it between the drunk's thumb and forefinger, and light the other end, Akiona instructed. When the fire got to his hand, the drunk would wake up. And carry a blister for a few days.

That first night I had another lesson. As we crossed the bridge to River Street, Akiona stopped me with his arm and asked, "Do you see what I see?" It was a horse running loose. It looked to me like a very ordinary horse, but it meant more to the veteran cop.

"Every time you catch one of those," he said, "you get five bucks. The stableman is glad to pay it."

Akiona ran out and grabbed a rope hanging from the horse's neck. Within half an hour a stableman had answered our call and had come to pick up his horse, and Akiona handed me a five-dollar gold piece. I was perfectly willing for him to keep it all since he had caught the horse, but Akiona insisted we whack it up fifty-

fifty and suggested we drop by a Chinese restaurant to make change and have dinner.

A lean Chinese came to our table quickly. Akiona introduced him to me as Chow Me Fat and told him I was a new policeman and would be on the beat. Today, the sons and daughters of men like Chow Me Fat speak English as well as anyone else in the islands. Some speak like Harvard graduates, which, in fact, they are. But in those days there were many Chinese who gave their own twist to our island pidgin.

"You teachee him good," Chow told Akiona. Then he launched into a tirade against another cop.

"When I blow whistle, you come quickee," he urged me. "You no be allee samee dat fella. Eli time I blow whistle, he no stopee. Trouble tom, no can find, but eat tom come, he allee tom come. Me thinkee he no likee workee."

The talkative Chow, with some head-shaking, worried because Akiona wouldn't be around on the next soldiers' payday, which, I gathered, was always a fairly exciting day of the month. Then he asked us what we wanted for dinner. I ordered a beef sandwich and coffee. Chow objected.

"No, no. You eatee steakee. Anything you likee. You no pay. Kau kau flee."

Akiona put in, "Come on, John, eat up. Everything's on the house."

So I ordered a small steak, French fries, and coffee.

"You allee samee solja," Chow told me. "Eli time, steakee, Flench fly, slice tomaty."

I wasn't having tomatoes. Yet I was to find out that what Chow said was true. Why, I don't know, because I've never heard there was any shortage of steak in the Army even in those days. But every soldier who came to town ordered steak with French fries and sliced tomatoes.

While Chow was getting our orders, Akiona explained that officers even from the River Street beat came down here to eat free. The Chinese proprietors didn't mind because they needed plenty of help on Army paydays.

Then the veteran policeman warned me, "Whatever you do, don't be as greedy as the cop who had this beat before me. He wasn't satisfied with having free meals when he was on duty. He'd come around on his off-duty hours. Then he even got to bringing some of his friends. The restaurant owner warned him, but he paid no attention. So someone turned him in to the captain and now he's pounding a beat on the other side of town where there aren't any restaurants."

When we checked in that night, Captain Fieldgrove asked me when my uniform would be ready. I told him I was picking it up in the morning. In that case, he replied, the next night would be my last with Akiona. Thenceforth I'd have a beat of my own. Training was quick in those days. A lot depended on the individual officer. Today the cop on the beat has to follow the book more closely. In those days he was allowed considerably more latitude in making decisions. I got an example the next night with Akiona.

We were passing a massage parlor on our way to the Chancre Barn when an argument attracted our attention. A husky gentleman, somewhat in his cups, was berating the proprietor. When we stopped, he turned to me, apparently thinking I was a detective because I was not in uniform.

"My name's Bill O'Toole," he began. "This guy just gave me a sloppy massage. I asked for my money back and he won't give it to me."

I told him he was asking me to help him collect his money, and of course I couldn't do anything like that. If he wanted to, he could hire himself a lawyer and sue.

"To hell with a lawyer!" he bellowed. "I want my dough now!"

Just then Akiona said something, and O'Toole asked him what business he had butting in and grabbed him by the badge. Akiona dropped him with a short right to the chin and I grabbed him by the collar to haul him to his feet and put him under arrest for assaulting an officer. Under the circumstances, O'Toole probably felt he was the one assaulted. But that was the way such things went. I started walking him to the police signal box to call the patrol wagon when Akiona intervened. He took the battered one by the arm and gave him a lecture somewhat as follows:

"Listen, Mr. O'Toole. Your head looks a little square to me. It looks like it needs a little rounding out. Now I'm going to give you some advice. The next time you make any trouble on my beat, or do something like grab at my badge, I'm going to round out those square spots on your head. Ya get me?"

"Yes, officer," answered a much more humble O'Toole.

"All right," said Akiona. "Now beat it before I get mad."

Still the complete rookie, I reminded Akiona I had placed the man under arrest.

"Oh, forget it," said Akiona, smiling. "O'Toole's a good Irishman."

That night Akiona gave me a few last-minute tips of the sort you never get in books. They were to prove very valuable. For one thing, I ought to carry a sack of Bull Durham tobacco "whether you smoke or not." My eyebrows must have gone up on that one. He explained quickly: "Suppose you get tangled up with more men than you can handle. You get some Durham in your left hand, your club in you right. Then put yourself in position with the wind at your back. When the moment comes, you throw the Durham into their eyes with a sweeping motion. Their eyes will smart, and the first thing they'll do is start rubbing. Now you have your feet, your left fist, and your club all working. Before they know what hit them, you'll have them on the pavement or hurt enough so they won't resist any more."

He had some other close-combat tips. On the use of the club, he advised, "Don't use your club on their heads. Hit them on the side of the neck where the neck meets the shoulder, or on their arms either below or above the elbow, or jab them with it in the solar plexus." On using the feet, he said, "Never kick anyone anywhere except on the shins. If it gets to the point where you have to use your shoes, never kick with the toe. You might miss. Always use the sides of the soles. A slight tap is enough. They'll feel it."

The following Monday I wore my new uniform and for the first time felt more like a cop than I had until then. In my new blue coat and white trousers I got a little ribbing from the other officers as they dressed, but underneath I could detect a sort of gentleness and fellowship that took the sting from the words.

An hour later, walking my new beat on King Street, the one Akiona had predicted for me, I didn't feel at all like a policeman, at least not an efficient one. The fact is I knew less about police affairs than any of the characters in the area I was supposed to keep in check and arrest on occasion. I had a few moments of stage fright but soon got over it. The most anyone could expect of me was my best, and I saw no reason why that wouldn't be good enough. After all, my hard-boiled yet gentle friend Holburn Akiona had been a rookie once.

As I walked my beat in the Hawaiian sunshine with the mixed aroma of fresh fish, Chinese spices, and the waters of dirty Nuuanu Stream in my nostrils, it wasn't long before I began to remember the advice I had received to take both mental and written notes of everything I observed. I made up my mind to study faces until I could recognize criminals as readily as I could members of my own family. There really wasn't much time for stage fright.

Little by little, I learned the ways of a policeman of those days. Some weren't according to the book, certainly, but they helped an officer do his job more efficiently and with less strain. Akiona was still my number-one teacher, for, though he wasn't on the beat with me, he had the River Street beat next to mine. We saw each other several times a day and moved to help each other when help was needed.

He taught me about the "alarm clock" for use while sleeping on duty. On Sundays, if the police were short-handed, we had to do a double shift of sixteen hours. My first Sunday, Akiona and I patrolled from 10:40 P.M. until about one o'clock in the morning. Then Akiona led the way back into an alley where he pulled a couple of boxes together and we sat down to have a midnight siesta. Before he dozed off, he set his "alarm clock." He took hold of his club, clenching the handle in his right hand with the length of the club lying loosely in his left palm. I did the same, and in no time at all we had both fallen asleep.

We were both awakened when Akiona's club slid out of his hand and fell end first on the cement of the alley. We looked at our watches and found we had slept only half an hour. There was still half an hour to go before we had to call in to headquarters. So we sat back again and Akiona "set" the "alarm clock" in his hand.

Some time later, I woke up to find it was 2:05 A.M. Akiona was still asleep, his club firmly in his hand. I left him there and went down to his call box and called in for him and then back to mine to make my own call. Akiona was still corking off when I came back to the alley. I sat for a while and smoked a cigaret. Still he didn't wake up. Then I went out on the street to walk our beats for half an hour. Everything was quiet. When I returned to the alley, Akiona was still asleep. I sat down on the box again and pretended to doze off. Just then Akiona woke up. He shook me hastily.

"Gee, it's 3:45! We're an hour and forty-five minutes late," he cried.

"What happened to your alarm clock?" I asked.

"Damn it, when you want the thing to drop, it doesn't. When you can sleep, the damn thing drops and wakes you up. Come on, we got to call in quick."

I let him stew until we got out to the street. Then I told him I'd called in for both of us already back at 2:10. He grinned with relief. But I saw you couldn't trust that alarm clock thing too far.

A couple of nights later, when I found two drunks sleeping in Hell's Half Acre, I decided to try one of those tricks Akiona had taught me. I wet the end of a couple of cigaret papers, stuck them between the thumbs and forefingers of the sleeping men, and set the dry ends on fire. When the fire burned down to their hands, the drunks came to life and began swinging their burnt hands. They were lying so close that they actually struck each other, and almost before I knew it, they were fighting, each accusing the other of striking the first blow.

I called the wagon and had them both booked for "detention," merely for safekeeping, to be turned out next morning when they were sober. But then and there I decided I wasn't going to "hothand" anyone else. Like some other methods used by callous police officers, that one was too cruel for me.

We used quite a few methods in those days that wouldn't work today. I tried one like that only a few nights after I'd been on the beat. It all started at the Chancre Barn. When I hit the dance hall that night, "Russian Nora," one of the proprietors, came up to me and complained about a seaman from a freighter inside giving the girls a bad time. When she had threatened to call the police, he had cussed her and the girls, then left. She gave me a pretty good description of him. He was a husky chunk of a man whose outstanding feature was a handlebar mustache.

Twenty minutes later, I actually collided with him when I rounded the corner of King and Liliha streets. He gave me plenty of grounds for an arrest by telling me off with some choice obscenities common to the seagoing men of that day. I put my hand on his shoulder and told him I was arresting him. He gave me a belligerent grin and snarled, "Take that dirty paw off me, flat foot," then reached up unceremoniously and took my hand off his shoulder.

So I took him more firmly by the arm and said, "All right, Mr. Handlebars, come along with me."

"Who are you calling Handlebars?" he shouted. "No one is going to call me Handlebars and get away with it."

He swung at me. I ducked and punched him sharply in the kisser, which stopped him for the moment. Then I got my fingers firmly into one end of his mustache and pulled him toward the call box where I called for the wagon. You couldn't have asked for a more docile prisoner. The handlebar hold had turned him from a raging lion into a mild and gentle lamb.

I rode along with him to the station, keeping my hold. Before long he was squealing like a stuck pig. I relaxed enough to let him bite a chew off a plug of tobacco he had. He was still very subdued when we got to the receiving desk. There his mustache got him into more trouble. The captain of the preceding watch was standing behind the counter. He was a dark Hawaiian who sported a walrus mustache of his own. He could not resist joining in the fun. He reached out, got hold of the prisoner's mustache and pulled, saying, "Come up here, Mr. Handlebars."

By that time the poor fellow's upper lip was so sore that he jumped too fast, struck the counter with his chest and spewed tobacco juice all over the captain. Whether he did it on purpose or not, none of us is sure to this day. The captain, with the joke on him, turned purple with rage. He hurdled the counter and started punching Mr. Handlebars. The rest of us pulled the enraged captain off before he could do any real harm. We finally convinced him the seaman hadn't let fly with the tobacco juice on purpose. After it was all over, we let Mr. Handlebars off without any charges.

My first soldiers' payday came the second month I pounded a beat. It gave me more action and excitement than anything I'd seen up to that time. Thousands of regulars from Schofield Barracks hit town that weekend looking for liquor and women and finding both, illegal though they were technically. The soldiers of that day were more mature than most of the young lads you see in the armed forces today. A lot of them were thirty-year men. Virtually all were in the Army because they liked that life better than anything else that was offered. Generally they were rough but good-hearted fellows who only wanted some entertainment. But plenty of them would as soon take a punch at a cop as look at him if they got riled.

Early in the evening, Akiona and I dropped around to our friend Chow, proprietor of the restaurant that fed cops free. We found him doing a rushing business with every soldier ordering steak, French fried potatoes, and tomatoes. While Akiona and I were in the kitchen drinking coffee, we could hear the steady cry from the waiters:

"Fly steakee!"

And the cooks yelled back, "All lai, all lai," and then to one another Chinese words that must have meant, "Tomaty! Potaty!"

I asked Chow, "Don't these soldiers eat anything else?"

"No, no," he exclaimed. "All tom steakee, even potaty nodda style no likee. Only fly potaty."

Everything was quiet. But we'd hardly left the place when a police whistle sounded from the restaurant. We hurried back. Chow with his whistle was standing out in front with a couple of the waiters. They were all yelling and waving with much excitement.

"Policeeman, you come quickee! Solja likee fightee. You go insigh quickee."

Inside, we found that one soldier had smashed a bottle of ketchup against the wall, spraying a couple others sitting at the table. When we asked him why he had done it, he gave us an answer typical of a lot of GIs of that day.

"I just wanted to get a rise outa you guys," he told Chow. "You always run and blow that whistle and get so damned excited."

We gave him a lecture, and after a bit Chow was pleading with us, along with the other soldiers, not to take him in. So we let him off. As we were leaving, Chow told us, "Latah you come back, eatee big steakee. You two good policeeman. You no come, solja bloke lesstablant."

Looking back, I can see that the Chinese of that day was in a hot spot whatever he did. If the soldiers weren't giving him a bad time, young fellows like myself were pulling his strange-looking queue. He had a hard row to hoe.

No sooner had we left the restaurant than a soldier came to tell us about a phony bootlegger who had sold him a pint of what he said was *okolehao* (liquor made from *ti* roots) for three dollars. Only it turned out to be cold tea. Before we could get anywhere chasing the bootlegger, another soldier stepped up to complain about a man who had promised to get him a woman, had taken his three dollars, and then left him standing on a corner.

It happened that I knew the bootlegger from the description and I knew where he hung out. We went and picked him up there. Before we got all the way back to Aala Park to get the soldier to make an identification, we saw signs of action in the park. Someone told us a couple of soldiers were beating up a civilian.

We got there in a hurry to find that the two GIs had found the phony pimp and were working him over. We stopped the proceedings and took both the petty crooks down to book them for gross cheat, an offense for which each eventually did three months in the local jail. I guess we could have run the soldiers in for taking the law into their own hands, but we didn't. In those days a policeman made up some of the law as he went along. I doubt that any less justice was dispensed than is today.

3

First Year on the Beat

SOLDIERS were rough in those days, but mainly they meant no harm beyond a scuffle. We of the police were not exactly lilies-of-the-valley, either, so we didn't mind an occasional bout with them. As long as it was nothing more than a bit of exercise on both sides, no charges were filed against anyone. One night, for instance, Akiona and I were patrolling River Street when we saw a couple of soldiers loitering there. We told them to move on.

"You think you're tough because you've got that uniform on," yapped the one nearest me. "Take if off and I'll show you how tough you are."

I had peeled and fought soldiers more than once on that kind of challenge. Nearly every policeman had. But that night I didn't feel like it. I let go a punch that must have had plenty of body, for it all but boosted the soldier over the retaining wall by the street and into Nuuanu Stream. His campaign hat sailed into the water. As soon as the soldier got his feet under him, he took off running and his buddy followed. Akiona and I just stood there laughing.

We police of that day often scorned use of our clubs so long as the odds in a physical contest were anything like even. We put much stress on skill with our fists and on our strength and endurance. We competed among ourselves. An episode from some years later, about 1927, will give the reader an idea of how we felt about fisticuffs.

Anthony Cathcart, a big Hawaiian, was heavyweight champion of the department. I used to train with him at a local gymnasium. When he wanted more training than he'd get in those off-duty sessions, I'd also go up a Hotel Street alley with him and we'd take off our coats and caps and trade punches with bare fists until he'd had enough exercise. Often as not, we'd be wiping blood from our lips and nursing swollen eyes as we emerged from the alley.

Once we staged a bootleg fight between Cathcart and the champion of the Fire Department, with a ring set up and all. The firemen's champion was a *haole* with very fast hands and some cleverness. But Cathcart was too strong and rugged and he knocked the *haole* out in short order. We cops collected our bets happily, ignoring the fact that fighting was then as illegal in Hawaii as murder—though perhaps not so distressing to the community.

Cathcart, incidentally, had one training angle I've never seen or heard of anywhere else. I pass it along for whatever use it may be to modern prizefighters. He would get a piece of new sole leather and chew on it interminably, on the theory that it would make his jaw stronger and less vulnerable to knockout punches. Whether or not it had any effect I couldn't say but Cathcart was a tough man to hurt.

I made a couple of what the trade calls "good pinches" about mid-year when early one morning I spotted two of the town's toughest strong-arm men in a car, along with some other roughs, near the intersection of College Walk and King Street. (For all its cultural connotation, readers should be reminded that College Walk was nothing like a collegiate lovers' lane. Down through the years, Honolulu's College Walk saw more crime of one sort or another than almost any other street in town.) Anyhow, these two gorillas would lie in wait along a dark street for some harmless-looking passerby, preferably three sheets to the wind. When they had spotted their victim, the larger of the two would step out behind him, throw an arm under his chin, and half-strangle him into unconsciousness, whereupon the two would go through his pockets.

I happened to recognize the pair among the five toughs in the car; they told Akiona and me they were "catching fresh air." We took in all five and started finding charges that fitted them. What the newspapers called "clearing up a wave of strong-arm cases" was really as simple as recognizing two wanted muggers. Still, I was learning it pays for a cop to develop a memory for faces.

An incident that required a little more energy began at two

o'clock one morning in June 1923 when I heard a pistol shot just after I had telephoned in from the police call box at King and River streets. The shot was followed immediately by the sound of running footsteps. The steps were coming my way, so I stepped into a passageway between tenement houses and waited. A man appeared, running across Pauahi Street toward me. When he got close enough, I stepped out and grabbed him. Before I could ask him anything, he gasped out that someone up on River Street near Kukui had tried to hold him up. My fugitive said he had run and the holdup man had taken a shot at him.

It occurred to me that I had wandered off my own beat and was on Akiona's. I hadn't seen Akiona since 12:30, and now I had a man to turn over to him. I remembered there was another police call box at the corner of River and Pauahi streets, so I told my man to come along and we headed that way. Somehow, for no particular reason, I began to get suspicious of this lad. I asked him if he objected to a search. He said he didn't and I went over him from armpits to the cuffs of his trousers. There was nothing suspicious on him.

But when we got about fifteen feet from the call box, he made a dive for a nearby garbage can. When I caught up with him, he was fumbling and digging for something. Suddenly I realized it must be the gun. I grabbed him by the collar of his shirt and the seat of his pants and up-ended him into the stinking garbage, jamming him down head-first as far as I could and holding him there. In a moment he was fighting as hard to get out as he had trying to get in.

When I decided he'd had enough asphyxiation to subdue him somewhat, I kicked over the garbage can and pulled him out, all festooned with remnants of chop suey and fried shrimp, making sure he had no gun in his hand. He appeared interested only in getting air into his lungs and remained entirely cooperative while I called the patrol wagon.

The wagon came and I loaded him in, then asked the driver to wait while I searched through the garbage. It wasn't a pleasant task, but presently I came up with what I'd expected to find—a 32-caliber revolver. I got in the wagon and went along to the station. There the captain told me Akiona had found a man lying unconscious, with a bullet wound, and had taken him to a hospital.

"I think I've got the man who fired the shot," I told the captain. I explained about the garbage can fracas and showed him the revolver.

"Is this your gun?" the captain asked the prisoner.

"No, indeed, I don't know a thing about guns," was the answer.

When Akiona came in, he said the wounded man had been in such serious condition that no statement was possible. That night Akiona and I sat in a restaurant drinking coffee and wondering if we'd have the job of pinning a murder rap on my friend of the garbage can. But it didn't work out that way. The wounded man recovered and lived to identify his assailant as the real holdup man. The result was a conviction for robbery in the first degree and a sentence of from five to twenty years in Oahu Prison.

The first political campaign I saw from a policeman's point of view came in the fall of 1923 when David K. Trask ran against Sheriff Rose. Of course other candidates were running for higher, more publicized offices, but the sheriff's race was the big one for any policeman. Both Republicans and Democrats brought troupes of Hawaiian musicians to attract people to their rallies. Each candidate was covered with flower leis before he spoke. The degree of popularity and financial backing he had was reflected in the number of pretty girls who paraded up to place leis around his neck and kisses on his cheek.

I discovered that the police department became for a few months a hotbed of political intrigue. Campaigners for Trask tried to lure the policemen, including me, with promises of the good deal their man would give if elected. As for me, I stuck by Charley Rose, the man who gave me my job. But I didn't make too much noise about it. Maybe that was just as well, for Trask won.

Just about this time I almost flubbed an assignment that nearly made me look as funny as the old Keystone cops of the silent movies. It was the case of the Chinese lady forger. For about five months in the latter half of 1923, a young Chinese woman had been passing forged checks at the local stores. In spite of some energetic attention paid by the Detective Division, she remained free and in operation. She was always described as an attractive young woman of about thirty, well dressed, often in a Chinese blouse and a black skirt.

On November 20, Captain Arthur McDuffie of the Detective Division got a tip that the girl he wanted was Florence Ho, alias Florence Hoki, alias Florence Quinn, local female "Jim the Penman," that is, a forger, with a record known to us. Some diligent checking here and there disclosed that a woman answering that description had been a hospital patient recently for an appendicitis operation but had already left the hospital. No one knew where she had gone.

More checking through the girl's doctor finally traced her to a room on the second floor of a Chinese society building on North Vineyard Street. Detectives visited her there, taking one of the victims of her forgeries, and he identified her. After a period of protesting her innocence, Miss Ho broke down and confessed but argued that she was too ill to be taken to the police station. Since it was already early night, Captain McDuffie agreed to leave her where she was for the time being. He stationed one of his detectives at the door and took everybody else back to the station.

About 8:30 P.M. I was called in from my beat and detailed to relieve the detective. It was a quiet night—at least until 1 A.M. when the woman's young daughter, who had been sleeping in the same room with her, awakened during the night to find her mother had disappeared. I investigated and discovered at a glance that she had escaped by sliding down a line made of two bedsheets tied together.

Sweating over the thought of having a prisoner escape from right under my nose, I hurried down to the nearest taxi stand and was relieved to get a tip right away. Someone had seen a taxi leaving the scene with a woman passenger. About 3 A.M. the driver returned. I questioned him. At first he didn't want to talk, but after a bit he admitted he had taken the woman in question to Asylum Road. She had given him a five-dollar tip to keep his mouth shut.

I went to the spot where the taxi driver said he had dropped the girl. She couldn't have gone far in her weakened condition, I reasoned, so I started looking around the area carefully for some sign that might give me a clue. Luck was with me. After a few minutes, I spotted a lighted window. Approaching, I saw the lady forger sitting in a chair in the room. The house turned out to be her brother's residence.

With considerable relief, I put Miss Ho under arrest again. She explained to me that she was in quite a bit of pain because in making her escape she had fallen a considerable distance. I called the ambulance and had her taken to the City Emergency Hospital (at that time located at the police station) where she was examined by physicians and transferred to the Queen's Hospital.

Miss Ho's escape and recapture seems a fairly small event today in the light of many more exciting crimes that have occurred since. But it was big news then. The papers played it on their front pages. Captain McDuffie told a reporter it was the most sensational case on record at the time. I tell it now partly to show Honolulu as it was then, a seaport with a small-town mind.

4

A Slight Case of Murder

ON the afternoon of Saturday, September 27, 1924, I was tossed slam-bang into my first murder case. A telephone call came to the police station reporting that the body of a murdered man had been found in his bathtub. According to the usual practice in those days, the detectives had gone off duty Saturday afternoon. Captain Walter Fieldgrove, in charge at the moment, dispatched me to make preliminary investigations.

When I got to the house at Kahanu Street, I discovered immediately why our informant had been so sure it was murder. The body of an elderly man, fully dressed in street clothes, lay almost submerged in foul, dirty water up to the chin; a small washboard floated level with his face. There were wounds on his head and face. A rawhide lariat cut deeply into his neck through a slipknot and was tied securely under his wrists and ankles. The tying job had been done in such a way that the victim, if alive when placed in the tub, could not have avoided strangling himself.

The murderer had made very sure of succeeding at his job. He had apparently beaten the old man into unconsciousness (or possible death) with some heavy object, then tied him up in such a way that any movement of revival would tighten the noose around his neck. Finally, he had put the victim in a tub full of water and so there was every chance he might drown. The callousness of the act gave me a prickly sensation at the back of my neck. The land of Aloha, the land of my birth, apparently had some citizens just as cold-blooded as any in the world.

Sam Hardesty, the neighbor who had first reported finding the body, had already identified the dead man. Mr. Hardesty was an old friend of the deceased, Rowland Boystep. He told me he had missed his friend and called at his home that Saturday afternoon to see him. He knocked at the front door. Getting no response, he went around to the rear where he found the back door open. He entered and walked through the house until he found the body. I could have identified Mr. Boystep myself. He was a wealthy retired businessman of English ancestry who had lived in Hawaii for many years and was known by sight to many people in Honolulu.

My first move was to throw open the windows and let in fresh air. The stink of death was heavy in the bathroom. Though murder was new to me, I could easily guess Mr. Boystep had been in the bathtub for several days. Next I found the instrument the murderer had used to beat Mr. Boystep over the head. I would have fallen over it if I hadn't seen it. It was a Stillson wrench lying by the bathtub. Then I found a crumpled, water-soaked legal document half-flushed down the toilet. It was a will recently drawn up by the murdered man, which cut off a son and a daughter, residents of Honolulu, and left his property to a nephew in England. In the front room I found the torn-off cover of the same document.

The bedrooms had been ransacked. Drawers had been pulled out. Luggage had been thrown open, searched, and left open. Even mattresses on the beds had been overturned in a frantic search for something. To me, the pieces fit into place. The murderer had searched for and found the will which he attempted to flush down the toilet. There was also evidence that Mr. Boystep, although seventy-one years of age, put up a vigorous fight for his life. I found bloody finger marks in the dining room and hallway leading to the bathroom. To top it all, there was evidence indicating the time of the murder. From the previous Thursday, bread and newspapers had accumulated on the front porch, unopened. Mr. Boystep had been seen last on Wednesday morning.

It seemed obvious to me that the murderer, despite his callousness, had been in a state of panic. Otherwise, why would he have attempted to flush a whole legal document down the toilet when he might have torn it in small bits and achieved his purpose of destroying it forever? Why would he have left the cover of the will in the front room, plain for everyone to see?

My number-one suspect that afternoon was George Boystep, the son who had been cut off in the will. Captain John R. Kellett arrived on the scene after I had made my investigations. He heard my report and agreed that young Boystep was the obvious suspect. He had photographs taken and the body removed to the City morgue.

An autopsy performed by Dr. Richard G. Ayer showed that death had come from strangulation, not from drowning or from blows with the Stillson wrench, which was the instrument with which the elder Boystep had been bludgeoned into unconsciousness. Dr. Ayer found that the rawhide lariat, a decoration Boystep had kept hung on the wall of his home, had been the instrument of death. The man was dead when placed in the bathtub.

On October 3, Captain Kellett took George Boystep into custody and charged him with first-degree muder. The speed with which the case had been solved by the police set a new record. George Boystep was convicted of first-degree murder at 11:30 on the night of December 3, 1924, after the jury had been out for four hours. Standing before Judge James J. Banks for sentencing, young Boystep still professed his innocence, but the judge commented, "You have had a fair trial before an intelligent and impartial jury. Every right which was yours under the law was accorded you. You were represented by competent counsel. The jury, after due deliberation, reached the conclusion that you are guilty and the court thoroughly approves the verdict. You committed a terrible crime. You took the life of the man who gave you life." Judge Banks sentenced young Boystep to life imprisonment.

No one knew better than I that many elements of the case had been laid in my lap by a panicky, avaricious amateur at murder. Likewise, if the report had come in at any time except late Saturday afternoon, I would never have been called out on the case at all. Nonetheless my work attracted attention in the department. Murder is the big crime for the policeman or detective. The following spring, while George Boystep was serving his first months in Oahu Prison, I was promoted to the Detective Division. Just eighteen months after I had donned the uniform of a patrolman, I took it off for the plain clothes of the detective. But I kept my uniform cleaned and pressed, ready for use, and it was a good thing I did.

5

Plain Clothes and Blacksnake Whips

T HE Detective Division, I found, was almost as new a world as the one I entered when I first became a policeman. It was the same for nine other young officers promoted with me. Under command of Captain John R. Kellett were now twenty-two detectives. There were five grades of detective, the pay scale running from $115 a month at the bottom (the fifth grade) to $160 at the top. I was considered lucky to jump from $130 as patrolman to $150 as a second grade detective. Some were even luckier. My friend John R. Troche had been hired as a second grade detective from the start and had never pounded a beat. It was the sort of thing that could happen in those days.

We worked from 7:30 A.M. to 4 P.M. with an hour off for lunch. Then we returned at 7:30 P.M. and worked until 11 or midnight. On Saturdays we worked through until 2 or 3 A.M. Sunday and then had the rest of Sunday off. That was the regular schedule. It was thrown out the window when emergencies came up. Then we worked as long as we could take it.

It sounds like a terrible schedule now, even to me, but those days when I was a very eager young beaver, bright-eyed and bushy-tailed, it didn't look bad at all. In fact, none of the ten of us, so far as I can remember, were anything but happy to get a crack at the job. The hours looked good to us because we'd get almost a whole day off a week. Not until 1932 did the police and police detectives get their hours reduced to eight-hour watches, and the patrolmen were given a day off a week.

The Detective Division, besides being one of the important nerve centers in the city, was full of characters the likes of which Honolulu will never see again. It was a cross-section of the population with a little something extra added. Often detectives were called upon to act as interpreters. Every man in the division could speak at least two languages. Mine were English and Portuguese. There was one dignified gentleman named Stein who could speak eight. He wore a white vest with a gold watch chain across it, thus looking more like a banker than a police dick, though he was half-tight most of the time. Drinking, however, never seemed to affect his facility with languages.

Inevitably, there were two Irishmen, both with experience before they came to Honolulu. John Nelson McIntosh had been born in County Meath, Ireland, and had served with the South African Constabulary before migrating to New Zealand where he was, at various times, a foot patrolman and a mounted trooper in Auckland. He had served with the Department of Justice at Greytown in Wairarapa before coming to Honolulu to join the force in 1923. McIntosh won a high reputation here quickly and served for years with distinction.

Thomas J. Finnegan, from Castlerea, Ireland, had joined the Royal Irish Constabulary at Dublin. But after he finished a six-months' apprenticeship and before he could be assigned to a station, he migrated to the United States and eventually to Hawaii, where he joined the police force as a foot patrolman in 1924. In six months, he became a second grade detective.

Another second grade detective was Juan Oxiles who served with the Philippines Constabulary before coming to Hawaii. Probably the smallest man on the whole force was Harry K. Noda, a quiet little man of Japanese ancestry who said little, looked half-asleep most of the time, and in fact missed very little that went on.

One who never let his work interfere with his domestic obligations was Kam Kwai. He had been a member of the force since 1910. He had a child for every year of service—thirteen—and every one hale and hearty. There was nothing superstitious about Detective Kam. He boasted that he did not burn punk and papers in the belief that there was bad luck in the number thirteen.

The really unique character of the lot was Detective Chang Apana, who was to become the model for author Earl Derr Biggers' Charlie Chan. Aside from the fact that both Apana and Chan were Chinese and both detectives in the Honolulu Police Department, there were few other similarities. Charlie Chan of the movies is a subtle character who solves mysteries with Confucian sayings, no force at all, and a pleasant smile. Chang Apana was rough and ready—rough with suspects and ready with a blacksnake whip for loiterers, toughs, and hoodlums on the streets wherever he might meet them.

He had been on the force twenty-four years already when I was a rookie cop pounding a beat, and the stories of his exploits were numerous. The criminal element always held him in healthy respect, perhaps more so than they would have a character like the Charlie Chan of the movies. A few years later, in 1931, Chang Apana was offered a pension after thirty-three years of continuous service. He scornfully rejected it.

"What do I want with a pension?" he asked. "I'm only sixty-seven years old and what would I do if I weren't a policeman? Chinese live a long time and some of them have been known to raise another family of nine at my age."

In 1924 Chang was the Grand Old Man of the Detective Division and as such entitled to special privileges. He was no longer sent out on "live" cases but remained at the station to supervise trusties assigned to clean up the place. The table in the detective room had an ornamental top made from black and white dominoes and mah jong pieces Chang and others had taken in gambling raids in Chinatown. He loved to sit around and tell stories of his old cases. Young men like myself liked to listen.

One of the tales he liked best was of how he captured two lepers named Kokuma, a man and wife, who had sucessfully evaded the police and had hidden themselves on the Kawaihapai* ranch of Walter F. Dillingham, one of the Territory's most famous businessmen. As Chang Apana told it, he was young and agile then, full of ambition and courage, and the assignment bore no terror for him even though it would be an arduous and dangerous job.† There

*Kawaihapai is the upland between Waialua and Kaena Point on Oahu. Jardine refers to the Dillingham Ranch at Mokuleia.

†One of the most controversial duties ever given the police in Hawaii was the apprehension of victims of leprosy who resisted being sent to the settlement on Molokai. The most publicized resistance on any island was that of a man named Koolau on Kauai in 1893. Hiding out in Kalalau Valley, he shot a sheriff who came after him, then single-handedly held off a military contingent equipped with a howitzer. He was never taken.

was no way to get up on the high slopes of Kawaihapai to effect a capture except through the tangled tropical brush. The Kokumas were known to be armed and determined not to be taken.

But they were not criminals, merely victims of the most feared malady in the Pacific, perhaps in the world. They would have to be taken with a minimum of violence. With four other officers, Chang Apana penetrated the brush in a stealthy approach through several miles of jungle. Apana was the first man to emerge in the clearing where a ranch cabin was located high on the mountain.

He spotted Kokuma sitting near the house, idling. The leper saw the detective at the same instant. He made a rush for the house and Apana ran to intercept him. They met and grappled before the door of the house. Kokuma got hold of a sickle. He cut Apana several times before the detective managed to overpower the leper and put handcuffs on him.

The detective's next move was to catch Mrs. Kokuma, a powerful woman, just as determined not to be taken as her husband. The woman had been sleeping, but Apana's footsteps awakened her. As he entered the bedroom, she sprang up to seize a rifle that was leaning against the wall. She dashed past him, her loose hair flowing behind her.

Apana was equal to the emergency. He made a grab for her hair, got a handful, and pulled her to the floor. The woman fought back until Apana was near exhaustion. She was subdued only when the four other officers finally arrived and helped take her into custody. The lepers were taken to the police station at Honolulu and then shipped to Kalaupapa Peninsula on the island of Molokai, then as it is today, Hawaii's leprosy settlement.

In this setting and with such colleagues, I began to learn the tricks of the detective's trade and to discover that they are not much different basically from those of the policeman. The principles were the same but the technique employed less brute strength and more brains. Just like the harness cops, the detectives built their own strings of stool pigeons. A man was only as good as his stool pigeons were.

I did the same thing, of course. I used the little fish to catch the big ones. In many cases when I picked up some small-timer for petty larceny, or the likes of that, I didn't charge him with the crime but put him under obligation to let me know anything he heard on the street. That's the system in Honolulu, and from what I hear, it's the system all over the world. I imagine the FBI and Scotland Yard have their stool pigeons just like any other agency of criminal investigation. Like any other detective, I had to have them. What would the police do anywhere without them?

One thing I learned quickly that some detectives miss is the importance of having a close liaison with the beat policeman. Too many detectives, I have discovered, consider themselves so far superior to the ordinary harness cop that they don't bother to find out from him the things he knows, things that often are essential to solving the case at hand.

This fact was impressed upon me in a case I had shortly after becoming a detective. A Chinese store on King Street had been burglarized, and I was assigned to the case along with a veteran detective. The only clue at the scene of the crime was a brown hat. The hat didn't mean much to my partner, but I had been on that street as a uniformed cop only a few months before. One glance at that hat and I knew the owner. I had seen him wearing it often enough when I was pounding up and down the street, sniffing the pungent odors of steamed shrimp and fried rice.

With this evidence, we quickly picked up our man and brought him to the station. My partner was skeptical at first, for our suspect had a shock of bushy hair. When we tried the hat on him, he let it stand up on top of his hair as if to say, "See, it can't be my hat." But I reached over and jammed the hat down over the hair and it fit like a glove. Within a few more minutes, the suspect was admitting that burglary and a few more. Perhaps he remembered seeing me on the beat as often as I'd seen him and knew there was no use trying to fool me any longer. From that time on, I have never ignored anything a beat policeman had to say about a case I was working on.

In 1925 I was one of several detectives assigned to a police experiment that would never happen today, though it was symbolic of

Hawaii at that time. It wouldn't be legal today, and I'm not sure it was legal then, but I wouldn't say it was unsuccessful, either.

It was a whipping squad organized to combat a rising trend of hoodlumism and crimes of violence rising from it. New gangs of young toughs had grown up and were hanging around street corners attacking servicemen, women, or anyone that might attract their attention as a potential victim.

Five of us were "armed" with blacksnake whips which we wore coiled around our waists. We were put in the charge of Sergeant Antone Louis and sent out to quell the roughnecks by giving them back something of their own medicine. Others on the squad were John R. Troche, Oliver Barboza, George Nakea, and Joe Munson.

Maybe we acted somewhat like bullies, for bullies were our chief targets, but to a considerable degree our action was effective in breaking up the gangs. Young thugs who felt like heroes fighting clubs and fists with clubs and fists squealed like naughty children when they were on the receiving end of blacksnake whips. And we were pretty good. We got so good we could flick small specks off the seats of hoodlums' pants.

Unfortunately for all concerned, Detective Oliver Barboza and another officer accidentally flicked the wrong youngster while pursuing a bunch of young hoods and were charged with assault and battery. They were convicted in district court and fined $100 each. The case was appealed to circuit court and the fine reduced by the judge there to $25. Captain Kellett paid it for them.

But the incident lent force to a campaign begun by a segment of the public to have whipping outlawed as excessively brutal. It was this same public, of course, which had been demanding action against the hoodlums only a few weeks before. Now the outcry was that we'd gotten too tough. Yet no one had been seriously hurt, and the hoodlums were being rapidly turned into peaceful, if not entirely exemplary, citizens.

Whips were never again used by the Honolulu police in such a way. Maybe it is a good thing, maybe a bad one. I do believe it kept a lot of young men straight who might have become dangerous criminals. And it didn't hurt them physically half as much as it hurt their dignity by showing them up as mischievous children rather than tough guys. I still believe it's better to whip a young man than to have to shoot an older one.

I like the old wisdom of Solomon when he said, "Withhold not correction from the child, for if thou beatest him with a rod, he shall not die. Thou shalt beat him with the rod, and shalt deliver his soul from hell."

6

When Time Almost Ran Out

I LIKED being a detective. Maybe from the start I liked being a detective too well. Or maybe I showed it too much. Maybe my luck was a little too good for a rookie, too. I felt that I was beginning to be the object of considerable jealousy among some of the older heads. Maybe the reporters were finding better copy in some of my cases than in some of the veterans' cases. In any event, I was convinced by the latter part of 1926 that I was not going to get anywhere in that climate and that I wouldn't even be very comfortable staying where I was.

So, despite the cut in pay, I asked Sheriff Trask for a transfer back to the rough-and-tumble of the Patrol Division. My request was granted. My superior was Captain Stanislaus Poaha and I was sent to pound the Nuuanu Street beat. I didn't have long to wait for action, more exciting action than I cared to find.

At two o'clock on the afternoon of September 9, 1926, I was browsing along between Vineyard and School streets, thinking very little and keeping my eyes open for some loudmouth roughnecks who had been reported in the area. Everything was quiet. I was about to turn and go back down Nuuanu when a car pulled to a stop across the street and the driver yelled, "Officer! Officer! Come here!" I hurried to the car. He said he had heard shots on School Street, passing Kauluwela School.

I jumped on the running board and asked him to drive me there. I could see he wasn't very happy about it. That section was in the middle of one of Honolulu's slums and as tough as any. Shots in the area might mean anything in the middle of the day. We reached School Street and headed for the location. From a distance of about a hundred feet, I could see a man out in the middle

45

of the street waving a revolver over his head. I had intended to ask the driver to keep his head down and charge the gunman with the automobile, but he had ideas of his own.

"Officer, this is as far as I'm taking you," he told me in a shaky voice.

I hopped off the running board. In no time at all, my driver had backed into a driveway, whipped his car around, and was heading back in the direction he'd come from. Now I had the problem of the man with the gun. As usual, I was not carrying a gun of my own. At the same time, children were leaving the school, standing on the street in clusters as children will, waiting to see what was going to happen. Older people with a greater sense of self-preservation were peeping out from behind board fences and hedges. A few were trying to wave the children off the street, and some were shushing the others, with their fingers to their mouths.

Well, there he was in the middle of the street, all mine. I wore the uniform. It was up to me to decide what to do with him. If he didn't decide first. He was a middle-aged Japanese man from his appearance. That was all I could tell about him. I put my hand on my right hip as I walked toward him in the sunshine, trying what I knew was a futile bluff, but he didn't make a move. He was facing me, watching me with apparent unconcern, the pistol held down by his side. I saw it was a Big Betsy, a 45 automatic of the type the U.S. Army uses, a weapon that knocks down with a slug any person it hits.

At closer range I could observe the details of his appearance—his black disheveled hair, his mussed white shirt, his eyes looking at me with the lack of focus of those emotionally or mentally deranged. He raised his left hand toward me in a forbidding gesture and turned his head to look briefly at the women and children on the sidewalk. I began thinking of God about the time I was within twelve feet of him. I tried to say a prayer for both him and me. I felt we were both likely to be judged by Him in the next few seconds.

The Japanese was looking up in the air now, and he had drawn his left arm back to a bent position on his chest. I moved my hand from my hip as if I were pulling a pistol from a holster. His pistol hand began moving up and I thought, "Here it comes." He shoved the muzzle of the pistol in his mouth and pulled the trigger, then reeled backward and fell dead in the street. A pool of blood formed beneath his head.

I ran forward and picked up the pistol and ejected the shell. While I was examining them, a detective squad car came up. Detective Troche leaped out and asked for my story of what had happened. I knew very little more than he did. Together we set about finding out.

Our answer was in a clothes-cleaning shop about forty feet away where we found the body of a dead woman lying in blood on the floor. She had a bullet wound in the side of her head and another in her chest. Neighbors identified her as the man's wife. Witnesses said the married life of the pair had been marred by the wife's nagging. That was the only explanation we ever got of the murder-suicide.

When I wrote my report at police headquarters, I had to side-step the fact that I had had no gun on me during the confrontation. Maybe I should have worn one. The Nuuanu beat certainly proved more dangerous than the Detective Division.

That year, about eight o'clock one evening, I rode along with the patrol wagon to the old Moiliili Road to pick up a notorious Filipino character. The driver and I loaded him into the wagon. We had driven about two blocks when he suddenly lunged at me with a knife.

He caught me unawares. But his first slash was short and it merely grazed the front of my uniform coat, so close that his razor-sharp blade sheared the buttons off. They flew upward like water spraying from a fountain, some of them striking me in the face. I still couldn't react. His second try was a thrust, stopped miraculously by the heavy leather of my police belt and the grace of God.

By then I had come alive. I caught his knife hand and turned the blade into the wire mesh of the side of the patrol wagon. At the same time, I jammed his head and face against the wire with my other hand. Then I punched him into submission. I must admit, by that time I had worked up considerable enthusiasm for the job. When I thought about it afterward, I realized that the only thing between me and a knife blade in my gut was that heavy leather belt.

Excitement kept coming my way even though I was assigned to the Fort Street beat in the heart of the business section. There a cop didn't have to work up a sweat to do his day's work, but I managed to anyhow—once, at least. This particular afternoon, while I was still at the station acting as call officer of the day, a complaint came in from Alexander Street about a man his neighbors said was threatening to kill his wife. In no time at all, I was on my way. When I reached the residence and rapped on the door, a man opened it and jammed the muzzle of a 45 right in my stomach.

"Do you have a warrant?" he demanded in a voice that showed his high emotional state.

I assumed as much calmness as possible and answered, "No, but I don't need one now with that gun on me."

By this time the door was open and I could see the wife sitting inside crying, cradling a small baby in her arms. I had learned that the only way to make any headway with a man as upset as this one is to keep as cool as possible and try to get him to do the same. The old Hawaiian saying "Cool head main thing" applied perfectly to situations of this sort. If you know a man is not a desperate criminal and can get him to listen to reason, you may be able to set him back in the orderly, law-abiding pattern of his life as he lived it until he suddenly got upset.

So I told this man he was acting very foolishly. I told him there was no sense in using a gun. After all, we had no complaint against him specifically about the gun. He wasn't even under arrest. I pointed out these things to him and suggested he put the gun down while we talked over his troubles. Just as I finished my little lecture, his wife called my name and I recognized her. She had been a neighbor of mine when we were small children. The sign of recognition seemed to do something to the man.

"Do you know my wife?" he asked.

"Sure," I told him, and went into the circumstances a little, stretching my explanation as long as possible to give time for the tension to relax. Already I felt the pressure of the pistol in my stomach growing less. Finally, I wound up with, "Give me that gun and let's talk this thing over."

He handed me the pistol. I looked into it and found it empty. I then shoved it into a pocket and sat down to hear the troubles of the couple. Their difficulty was strictly of a minor nature. Within a few minutes after I'd been standing there with a gun shoved in my stomach, I was acting as a marriage counselor. They sat and listened soberly. The upshot was that I didn't make any charge against him but walked away and let them work out their own problems.

Next day the man called the captain to say he didn't want the gun back, that it could be given to any policeman who needed one. The man had had enough of his splurge at violence and wanted no more of it. In later years we became good friends, and so far as I know the marriage continued successfully with no more quarrels that led to calls for the police.

On January 2, 1927, David Trask was succeeded by David Desha as sheriff. Captain Kellett left the Detective Division in accord with the wishes of the new sheriff. Michael Morse was appointed in his place. Later in 1927 David Desha resigned and Morse returned to the Traffic Division as sergeant. Charles E. Cassidy, Deputy City and County Attorney, was assigned by City and County Attorney Charles S. Davis to assume command of the Detective Division pending reorganization of the department. Also in 1927, Patrick K. Gleason took office as sheriff and David Hao became his deputy and captain of detectives.

All of this reorganization had its effect on me because, under Sheriff Gleason, I was again placed on the staff of detectives with the rating of detective, first grade. This time I worked hard and kept my mouth shut. In addition to my own pickups, I also kept track of all the pinches made by the other dicks, learning who was being arrested for what. I began keeping notes on all persons being sent to prison. I even visited them there to win their friendship and, in varying degrees, their confidence. Sometimes they would confess crimes to me that they hadn't confessed when they were sent up. I was able to clear up a lot of cases that way. From prison inmates, too, I often got the names of people on the outside who knew about a crime or might have been involved in one. More and more I learned to cultivate a relationship of trust with the men in prison, many of whom I sent up myself. It might surprise a layman to know how many criminals hold no grudge against the cop who catches them.

7

The "Boston Burglar"

THE "Boston Burglar" is the title of an old hillbilly tune, but the words had quite a different association for Honolulu in 1930. It all started in the Boston Building, one of Honolulu's modern office buildings of the time, located on Fort Street in the heart of the business district. One night, Leon Stan-Leigh, a watchmaker, was working there alone in his small shop. The only noise to be heard was of his own making as he poked and probed gently into the interior of an ailing timepiece.

Suddenly he was conscious of other noises. The watchmaker's fingers stopped poking. He listened. Sure enough, somebody was moving around in the next-door office of Dr. G. R. Marsily. But Dr. Marsily was away on the mainland. Besides, it was near midnight. Whoever it was must be taking advantage of his absence to burglarize his office. On tiptoe, the watchmaker went to the office door and looked in. He saw movement and the silhouette of a man.

With the utmost care, Stan-Leigh took off his shoes, left his office, and padded quietly downstairs and out of the building into the warm Honolulu night to search for a policeman. Luck was with him. Or so it seemed at the time. Not half a block away he found two officers at the corner of Fort and Hotel streets.

Together, exercising less caution now, the trio climbed the three flights of stairs and walked down the hall. Stan-Leigh tried the door of an office adjoining Dr. Marsily's business suite. Again he saw the movement of a man's figure against the light from a window. The burglar must have been moving from office to office.

"There he is!" the watchmaker shouted.

Before the cops could answer, two shots blasted through the

office door and Stan-Leigh got a smell of death. One bullet grazed his chin, the other his left cheek. The startled watchmaker turned to see what action the policemen were taking to catch the burglar. They had disappeared. He heard only the sound of running footsteps. Another shot sounded. The footsteps only ran faster.

Stan-Leigh proved himself of sterner stuff. He stood guard beside the door for half an hour waiting for the policemen to come back. When they didn't, he went back outside, where he found the cops and J. H. Thompson, superintendent of the building, waiting together. The police had raced out so fast they'd locked themselves outside by slamming the door. Then they had to find the building superintendent to get back in. But they were in no hurry. They said they were waiting for reinforcements.

As Thompson told the story later, the whole group then climbed the stairs again. Thompson unlocked the office door, whereupon one of the policemen drew his revolver, brushed Thompson aside and charged into the office firing several shots. Later, these shots were discovered to have broken several windows, doing little damage to the burglar, of course, since he had long since left the scene.

Nor had the traveling Dr. Marsily been the only victim of the criminal, who was soon to become known throughout the Territory as the "Boston Burglar." Detectives discovered that two other offices had been entered. A dentist on the same floor had lost $800 and the office of a Christian Science practitioner had been entered, though nothing had been taken.

The story was all over town the next day. The *Star-Bulletin* managed to be first on the editorial draw a couple of days later, with a condemnation of the two timid policemen. Their editorial ended: "Crooks who use guns must be met by guns in the hands of policemen who won't run."

That was only the beginning. *The Advertiser* next day opened all stops in a sarcastic editorial entitled, "Let's Have More Medals." Here's what the editorial said: "In addition to the medals for heroism proposed for members of the police force who performed distinctive service during last week's flood, a grateful community might just as well, while it is at it, arrange for casting two more emblems to be known as Safety First Medals, to be given to the uniformed heroes of the Boston Building robbery on Monday morning. . . . Such gallantry in the face of an emergency certainly deserves public acknowledgement, particularly in view of the fact that the police were a mere two to one against the burglar. Undoubtedly, had it not been for the quick thinking and prompt action of the officers in question, the thief would have outwitted them and been captured."

The Advertiser, remember, was one of the two most powerful newspapers in the Territory. Something had to give, and it did. A couple of days after the editorial, Sheriff Gleason fired the cops, charging them under a section that provided dismissal for any officer who failed to do his duty. Pat Gleason gave detailed reasons for the firing. But that didn't get the heat off him and the department.

A day or so after the discharge of the two policemen, the *Star-Bulletin,* the other powerful paper, came back with an editorial to remind the public as follows: "Now that the Police Department has unburdened itself of at least two officers who prefer to run in the opposite direction when a lawbreaker opposes them, it might be a good idea to capture the burglar in question, as well as others who have been making the city unsafe for life and property for so many months. . . ."

The *Hawaii Hochi,* a Japanese-English paper, got into the act, too, reminding readers: "It is not necessary to wait until a policeman has shown the white feather with possible tragic consequences to innocent people. There are tests that can be applied which will definitely prove the moral caliber of a man and show whether or not he has a yellow streak."

The *Hochi* said the Civil Service Commission should have been able to tell by special tests whether the officers had enough guts to be policemen. That one still has me beat. To this day, I've never seen anyone who could predict how a cop or anyone else will react to danger of sudden death. But then the newspapers knew more about it than we did. To hear them tell it, they always do.

Pat Gleason did his best to get the wolves away from his throat. He got a chance when a couple of vice characters named Tony Scanilo and Phil Chartard were arrested in an opium den at

Hauula. Gleason told the newspapers he was "practically convinced" Scanilo was the man who had chased the police in the Boston Building.

The catch was that nobody would ever know for sure, because the two were being floated to the mainland by the next steamship rather than making them serve six-month sentences for being present where narcotics were being used. It was a way of getting rid of undesirables in those days. The editors were not convinced that Scanilo was the Boston Burglar even though he had a couple of imposing aliases and had been a pug. Sheriff Gleason was asked by the press if it wouldn't be better to keep Scanilo in jail and try to crack him on the burglaries.

"Oh, you can't make him talk," Pat said. "He's an old-timer. It's better to get rid of him than to keep him here."

The reporters doubted that Gleason believed Scanilo was the burglar. They were right. The chase continued. By mid-December it had turned toward a Hawaiian on the island of Maui. When they chased him down, they discovered he had never left the island and therefore couldn't have committed the burglary. By this time, the tom-toms were beating harder than ever for somebody's scalp, preferably the Boston Burglar's.

Then things went from bad to worse. The Civil Service Commission heard an appeal from the two timid cops, overruled their firing by Gleason, and put them back on the force. They were pounding my old beats at Pauahi and River streets by the time Gleason called in Black, another detective, and me and told us to catch the burglar.

What Pat Gleason didn't know was that we had already been working on the case. At the civil service appeal hearing, we'd noticed that one witness had spoken of a young Chinese who had stood in front of the Honolulu Sporting Goods Company shortly after the burglary. The sporting goods store was near the Boston Building. Black and I decided this young Chinese might well be the burglar, watching quietly while the police ran this way and that hunting for him.

There had also been some burglaries in the Young Hotel Building only a couple of blocks away. We wondered if there might be a link between the two. Checking, we discovered that a young Chinese who registered as "Edward Akiona" had stayed at the hotel from November 5 to November 25. The description the clerk gave us, along with samples of his handwriting from the register, made us think he might be Edward Chung, a young man implicated in passing bad checks.

Centering on Chung, we found acquaintances who recalled that he had spent plenty of money following the recent downtown burglaries. He had registered as "James Lee" at the Blaisdell Hotel, as "Edward Akiona" at the Senator, and had bought plenty of expensive clothes. Chung's front was that he managed an electrical store in Hilo.

Next, we found an elevator operator at the Young Hotel who told us Chung was in the habit of going out late wearing old clothes, and returning at irregular hours. One such night, we learned, was the night of the Boston Building burglary. A day or so later, he had bought an expensive suit and a topcoat and then left for Hilo.

That was pretty strong circumstantial evidence. Pat Gleason took what we had and dispatched Deputy Sheriff David Hao to Hilo to find Chung and arrest him. Hilo police picked up the young Chinese as he was walking into the palatial old Hilo Hotel where he was staying in his accustomed luxury. Under questioning, he broke down and confessed to the Boston Building burglary and a string of other burglaries in both Honolulu and Hilo.

The ship bringing him back docked in Honolulu at 6 A.M. while it was still dark. The young man seemed in far better shape than Deputy Hao, who had come down with seasickness. He was happy to turn Chung over to Black and me. There followed an informal press conference during which the burglar played a starring role and we were the spear carriers. Young Chung, dressed in a natty gray topcoat and a blue serge suit, looked just like what he told reporters he had been, a junior at the University of Hawaii. He talked freely about the shooting at the Boston Building saying he hadn't intended to do more than scare away his pursuers and didn't realize until later how well he had succeeded. "It was a great life while it lasted," he told reporters.

Chung was known as a bright student by his teachers and a pleasant companion by the other students. He liked to play the bountiful host and as a result spent so much money that his family on Maui cut off his allowance. Some of his fellow students helped him along until, unknown to them, he started the burglaries which provided him with plenty of cash thereafter, until his capture. He also wrote bad checks which he would make good with the proceeds from his burglaries. The last time he'd gone to Hilo, he had left $300 with a friend to take care of unpaid bad checks and debts.

The case was processed quickly. Chung pled guilty to three counts of burglary, although he had confessed to forty-seven burglaries in Honolulu and five in Hilo. Judge Charles S. Davis sentenced him to serve sentences running concurrently from five to twenty years.

We cops, who had been blasted by the newspapers only a few weeks before, now became heroes. The *Star-Bulletin* began an editorial: "We congratulate Sheriff Gleason, Deputy Hao, and Detectives Jardine and Black upon the capture in Hilo of the man believed to be the Boston Building burglar. The work of these individuals stands out in marked contrast to that of the patrolmen who, with the burglar virtually in their clutches, let him get away. . . ."

Next day *The Advertiser* handed Black and me the roses. Its editorial ran: "City Detectives Jardine and Black did a splendid job in uncovering the trail of the 'Boston Building burglar,' an accomplishment whose merits are accentuated by the earlier mishandling of the case by the Police Department high command. . . ."

There were times later, when the breaks went against us, that I wished those editors had remembered those editorials. But that's all part of being a cop.

8

The Night That Shook Hawaii

THE Massie case, an alleged rape followed by a murder, has inspired more lies, in my opinion, than even the bombing of Pearl Harbor. Lies about the case and the principals in it were cropping up all through the period 1931–1932 when the crimes occurred and the cases were tried in court. The truth was sensational enough. It got blown up almost beyond recognition by newspapers and magazines on the mainland until the impact of their volume alone influenced American thinking about Hawaii.

As it happened, I had a front row seat for the opening act of the Massie case. That year we were operating at a temporary headquarters at King and Alakea streets because of remodeling at our regular headquarters at Bethel and Merchant streets. I was the detective in charge of the division for the watch beginning at midnight, September 12, 1931, and ending at 8 A.M., September 13, a historic period in our history. But it started as just another Saturday night to me, and fairly lively, as expected.

I hadn't been on duty an hour before a husky, half-Hawaiian woman drove up to our headquarters with a bleeding ear, fire in her eyes, and a complaint to file. Detective Cecil A. Rickard took her complaint. She was Mrs. Homer Peeples, wife of a barber at Luke Field out by Schofield Barracks. She said she and her husband had been driving home from a party less than an hour before, when an incident occurred that spoiled their party mood entirely. At the intersection of King and Liliha streets in Palama, another auto had come sailing through a stop sign and almost caused an accident. The cars barely missed each other. Both came to a stop.

"Why don't you look where you're going?" Mrs. Peeples sang out.

Her husband started the car. At that moment, someone swore viciously in answer from the other car. Mr. Peeples stopped again. A muscular Hawaiian got out of the other car and came walking back.

"Get that damn *haole* off the car and I'll give him what he's looking for," he yelled at Mrs. Peeples.

She had done the talking so far. Besides, the Hawaiian was coming toward her side of the car. Mrs. Peeples was not one to get her husband to fight her battles, so she got out to meet the Hawaiian. As he came on, she pushed him back, noting with a side glance that another man, who looked Japanese, was getting out from behind the wheel of the other car.

The Hawaiian took advantage of her distraction by striking her heavily on the ear with his fist. Mrs. Peeples staggered back from the blow, then recovered quickly. She grabbed the man by the throat with her left hand and drove a hard right to his face. She said he seemed discouraged and started back to his car. So did the Japanese. Mrs. Peeples got in her car and directed her husband to drive to the police station.

A pretty careful observer, she had noted there were four men in the car. More important, she had memorized the license number: 58–895. That number was destined to be printed all over the country, but at the moment Rickard had no reason to give it other than routine treatment.

Mrs. Peeples was sent from the police station to the emergency hospital for treatment of her lacerated ear. At 12:50 A.M. Rickard broadcast the license number to police radio patrol cars with instructions to pick up the vehicle and the men riding in it. An hour and two minutes after Mrs. Peeples had made her complaint, the telephone rang in my office.

"John," I heard, "this is Captain Hans Kashiwabara at the receiving desk. I just got a call on an assault case. Will you send someone out to Kahawai Street to interview the complaining witness?"

I hung up and looked around. The detectives were all out on

cases so I went across the hall to the radio broadcasting room and arranged with Rickard to have a radio patrol car sent to the address, which was in Manoa, an exclusive part of town. The officers were to notify me of their findings. Shortly afterward, two detectives came in from their assignments, and I sent them to the Manoa address.

Less than half an hour later, one of the officers of the radio patrol called to ask me to go on the case myself. He said a Mrs. Thalia Massie had been brutally beaten and raped off Ala Moana Boulevard. I called Captain John McIntosh, head of the Detective Division, reported the request, and hitched a ride with a cop to Manoa.

When I arrived at Kahawai Street, the radio patrol officer who had called me told me what had happened up to the moment. When they got to the address about 2 A.M., he was met by Lieutenant Thomas Massie, a young Navy officer, who told him his wife had been beaten by a gang of boys and criminally assaulted. The officer then went inside to where Mrs. Massie was lying on a couch. He questioned her. The officer said the young woman had been beaten about the face and that she was hysterical and crying all the time he questioned her. But she managed to give him an account of what had happened.

She said she had been at a party at the Ala Wai Inn* in the Waikiki end of the city and had gone for a walk to get some fresh air. She had walked toward Waikiki on Kalakaua Avenue and turned right down John Ena Road.

After she had gone a short distance from Kalakaua Avenue, an old-model Ford or Dodge touring car had stopped alongside her. Two boys got out, grabbed her, and dragged her into the car, striking her at the same time. The car had then been driven to a spot along Ala Moana Boulevard, then turned off into the bushes, where the boys had all assaulted her. There had been five or six boys, she said, and all of them appeared to be Hawaiians. She did not think she could identify any of them, but she might possibly be able to identify their voices. The radio patrol officer asked Mrs.

*The Ala Wai Inn was located on the *makai* side of Kalakaua Avenue just above the Ala Wai Canal on the way to Waikiki.

Massie if she knew the license number of the car driven by her attackers.

"Of course not. How could I?" she answered.

I saw a police patrol wagon parked opposite the Massie house. A white man wearing white clothes was seated inside the wire-mesh enclosure in custody of the substation officers. He looked somewhat mussed and disheveled and a little subdued at the moment.

The substation police officers said the prisoner had been walking along lower East Manoa Road. The cop stopped and asked the pedestrian his name. He gave his name as Lieutenant Jack Archer. Other than this, he had given nothing but curt replies. Well, a man in his cups who talks like that to a cop, even if he's fairly well dressed in a white linen suit, is asking to get arrested, if for nothing more than suspicion of mopery [another word for loitering and vagrancy].

Then a patrol officer riding along with the substation officer pointed out aloud that the man's trouser fly was open. With as much dignity as possible under the circumstances, the man in the road buttoned up. But he still refused to cooperate. When he saw he was really going to be taken in, he came out with, "I want you to know I am an officer in the U.S. Navy with the Shore Patrol."*

If he thought that was going to be any big help, he couldn't have been more wrong.

"What!" exclaimed the cop. "You're on Shore Patrol and you talk like that to a police officer?"

No sooner had they picked him up than they ran into the radio patrol car sent to the Massie house. At that point, they heard about the rape case. Now they remembered that unbuttoned fly and wondered if maybe they didn't have the number-one suspect right in their wagon. The woman had spoken of five or six Hawaiians. But maybe she had her own reasons for telling that kind of story.

That was the beginning of the widely circulated rumor that Thalia Massie had had an affair or a fight or both with a naval officer who was a friend of her husband. The story spread by word of

*The Shore Patrol acts as Navy police on and off military bases. They are supposed to cooperate with local police and vice versa.

60

mouth from coast to coast. It's no wonder. I know police officers who were on duty that night who believe and retell the story about Mrs. Massie and the naval officer. A woman from San Francisco I spoke to recalled that she heard the story from a former governor of the Territory when he was on a trip to the mainland.

There was something else I learned later from the radio patrol officer's report. While he was in the house conversing with Lieutenant Massie, the officer whispered the license number, 58–895, of the car involved in the Peeples' case. Mrs. Massie was lying on the couch a few feet away. Could she have overheard and remembered the number? Or had her husband remembered and told it to her? Officials investigating the case were to wonder about that later.

When I went into the house, the agitated couple were still in the same room, Mrs. Massie on the couch, her husband trying to console her. She was a girl of only twenty, rather pretty, I was to discover in time. That night, though, her face was swollen from the beating. She was still sobbing, suffering from the shock of whatever had happened to her and from the tension in the room filled with police officers and Navy friends who had heard of the affair and had come over.

Lieutenant Massie appeared to be little more than half-conscious. He was somewhat under the influence of liquor he had drunk at a party they had attended earlier that evening, and his anger and frustration left him hardly a rational man.

Under the circumstances, I decided not to try interviewing either of them then. They had told their stories and any further questioning would have been a torment. Instead, I suggested we take Mrs. Massie to the emergency hospital for an examination of her injuries and any immediate medical aid she might need. I had in mind, of course, the necessity of a vaginal examination by a doctor to establish some kind of solid facts about the story of rape.

"Mrs. Massie," I asked, "would you please come with me to the hospital?"

"I don't want to go! I don't want to go!" she said, shaking her head.

She was half-hysterical. Rather than press the question myself, I drew her husband aside and told him how important it was for us to have an examination made. He talked with his wife for a few minutes and she consented to go. The Massies went on ahead. I stopped for a moment to tell the two detectives I had assigned to the case to remain on watch at the house. Several naval and police officers stood around outside, and the lieutenant arrested earlier was still in the patrol wagon. Mrs. Massie saw him and recognized him.

Then occurred a couple of incidents which may or may not have meaning in the case. What one of the detectives heard Mrs. Massie say to the naval officer in the patrol wagon was, "It's all right, Jack." After we had left for the hospital, the detectives at the house reported later, one of the naval officers started talking to them, telling them that the officer under arrest had left the party. But his fellow officers eased him away before he finished what he wanted to say.

While Dr. David Liu was examining Mrs. Massie at the emergency hospital, I took advantage of the wait to interview Lieutenant Massie and, later, the lieutenant who had been brought along in the patrol car. Massie told me that he and his wife had had four after-dinner guests that night—the naval officer under arrest and his wife, and another Navy couple. After each had a drink, they all went to the Ala Wai Inn using their family cars to make the trip.

It was a dancing-drinking party made up of young officers and their wives. The guests milled about here and there, so Massie didn't think much about it when he started looking for his wife between 11:30 P.M. and midnight and didn't find her. Lieutenant Archer couldn't find his wife, either, but there was nothing startling about that. The officers and their wives knew one another somewhat better than members of most social clubs.

Both husbands assumed their wives had already caught rides with friends for the next port of call of the evening, which was to be the home of a Lieutenant Rigby. That, too, had been prearranged. The Rigbys had invited everyone over to their house for a nightcap after they'd all had something to eat downtown following the party at the inn.

A little after 1 A.M., when Massie and Archer found themselves

62

without wives, they decided to drive to the Rigbys' in Massie's car. Archer had discovered his own car was gone. He assumed his wife had taken it to drive ahead. When they got to the Rigbys', they found no one was there. The door was unlocked, so they both went inside. Archer lay down on the couch and apparently fell asleep. Massie said he kept wondering where everybody was and whether or not he might have made a mistake about the meeting arrangement. He awakened the maid and asked if the Rigbys had been there. She answered in the negative. He decided to telephone his home to see if his wife might be there. Her answer gave him a shock that almost jarred him into sobriety.

"Something awful has happened, come home!" she cried in anguish.

He drove back to the house immediately, leaving Archer still apparently asleep on the couch. He found Thalia looking very much as she had when I entered the room later. She told him she had been beaten and assaulted. He immediately picked up the phone and called the police.

At this point I had one question, and I told him the answer was extremely important:

"Might it be possible that Lieutenant Archer could have attacked your wife?" I asked.

The question stiffened him, but he took it and answered directly, "That's absurd. Absolutely not."

Then, after reconstructing the evening again a little, he told me that, despite the confusion and milling around of guests at the party, Archer had never really been out of his sight for more than ten minutes at a time. He declared the thought was not only absurd but physically impossible.

The examination of Mrs. Massie by the doctor was still going on in the operating room, and so, standing by our car parked on Punchbowl Street, I interviewed Lieutenant Archer. His story confirmed Massie's at every point. Only he had not really been sleeping on the couch when Massie called home. He had heard his brother officer say on the phone that he'd be home in a minute; then he'd seen him dash out toward the car.

Archer reasoned something must be wrong. He roused himself

and decided to walk to the Massie house. He'd walked only a short distance when he stopped to urinate. After all, no one was around at that hour and even a naval officer could risk relieving himself without damage to his reputation. Then he'd failed to button the fly of his trousers properly.

A little later, a car stopped beside him on the road, almost in front of a Japanese store. Archer hadn't sobered up as much as Massie. He told me the conversation with the police officer had been a little fast for him. He didn't recall exactly what he'd said or what the policeman said. He did know he resented being stopped and questioned because he felt he had committed no offense.

The next thing he knew, he was pushed into a car and put under arrest. Archer told me the police officer had then driven to a police call box and called for the radio patrol car, into which he was transferred. This car drove to the Massie house where he was later transferred again, this time into a patrol wagon. He was sitting in the patrol wagon when Mrs. Massie passed. Archer remembered her saying to him, "Oh, Jack! Why are you there?" Archer didn't recall saying anything to her. In fact he didn't have anything more to add to the information he had already given.

About that time, something happened which was to raise considerable conjecture and debate later. A patrol car drove up and stopped in front of the emergency hospital. Over the car's radio came the voice of Detective Rickard, speaking from police headquarters, saying the car with license number 58–895 had been picked up. The message was repeated, as was the license number, several times over the radio.

Navy officers dressed in civilian clothes were standing nearby, along with some other men, having followed us from the Massie house to the hospital. The radio in the patrol car was audible for some distance. None of them gave any outward sign of having heard the call or seemed to note any special significance to it. But lawyers, jurors, and the general public were to wonder about the effect of that radio call.

Dr. Liu finally finished his examination of Mrs. Massie. She had talked to both him and the nurse who had prepared her for the examination. To the nurse, she said she had been attacked by six

Hawaiian men and wasn't able to identify them because it was too dark. Her story to the doctor was a little more detailed. She said she had been walking along John Ena Road when a car with four to six men pulled up and stopped beside her. Two men jumped out, seized her, and dragged her in. They drove her to somewhere in the bushes where they all raped her. She told the doctor, too, that she wouldn't be able to identify them because it was too dark.

Dr. Liu found no positive evidence that she had been raped. The incident had occurred two hours before, according to her account. Since that time she had been home and douched herself. The doctor stated that, although he found no fresh abrasions or contusions, it was possible that she had been raped by as many as four men without showing any unusual marks.

The doctor found plenty evidence of beating, though. Her right cheek was badly swollen and her left cheek somewhat swollen. Her upper lip was swollen, too. When the doctor examined her jaw, he found it tender. He did not examine Mrs. Massie's whole body.

In the meantime, things were happening in other parts of town. A detective called the radio room and received instructions to pick up the car with license number 58-895, registered in the name of Ida at an address in Cunha Lane. The detective was told a bunch of boys had picked up a white woman on John Ena Road and taken her down to Ala Moana Boulevard and assaulted her.

The detective drove to Cunha Lane and found the car in the garage, its radiator still warm. He roused the household to fetch out the slender young son, Horace Ida. The boy's mother and his sister, a geisha at a local teahouse, said he'd been out in the car. Horace denied it. He said he'd lent the car to another Japanese boy but couldn't remember the name. Asked if there were any other boys along with the one to whom he'd lent the car, Ida said there were some Hawaiian boys whom he knew only by sight. The detective put Ida under arrest and brought him in to the station.

At police headquarters, Captain John N. McIntosh, chief of detectives, questioned Ida and the story began to change. The Japanese boy he had first mentioned gradually turned into two Hawaiians named Joe and Ben. Ida claimed he didn't know their last names. Finally, he said he didn't want to tell their names because the car had almost been in a collision and he was afraid of getting them into trouble.

Just about that time, I arrived with Lieutenant and Mrs. Massie from the emergency hospital and turned Mrs. Massie over to the captain. Massie and I waited in the detective squad room adjoining the captain's office while Captain McIntosh questioned Mrs. Massie and got the main points of her story again. Then he went outside and had Ida brought in.

The boy had no warning of what he was going to see or what was going to happen. At that moment, Mrs. Massie looked exactly like what she was, the pitiful victim of wanton brutality. One of her eyes was partially closed. Her lips were swollen and cut. Her jaw was swollen. Her hair was disheveled, hanging down and liberally spotted with pine needles. McIntosh played up the drama of the situation.

"There, look at your beautiful work!" he said in a voice of doom, as he pointed at Mrs. Massie's battered face.

They say Orientals are stoic. Maybe they are sometimes. But not Ida. He looked scared and his eyes popped.

"I didn't do it! I didn't do it!" he protested.

But Thalia Massie nodded her head slowly up and down. Then she asked Ida a few questions. Her first one was, "Do you know a boy named Bull?"

Some people, including high officials in Hawaii, have maintained privately that they never believed Mrs. Massie was raped at all, but that she received her injuries in a lovers' quarrel or domestic fight. To them, I would suggest they consider carefully her question about "Bull." She repeated it later in different forms. She had heard one of her attackers call another Bull, and she assumed it was the nickname of one of them. She was a mainlander, new to Hawaii, and she didn't know that "Bull" had for years been a local general term of address, like "Mac."

It has always seemed to me that her effort to attach the name to one of her assailants is proof of her sincerity. Had she been making up a tale, she would never have asked a question like that. Not that evidence in the case rested completely on anything so flimsy. There was plenty of other evidence.

66

During the questioning, Captain McIntosh called in a veteran policeman and described to him the route the attackers took. The policeman guessed that the old animal quarantine station* would be the most probable place for the assault to have taken place. McIntosh ordered him to go there and make a careful search of the location.

Some time later, while McIntosh was still taking Mrs. Massie's statement in written detail, the policeman returned with a small pocket mirror, two boxes of matches, an old handkerchief mildewed and filthy, an empty ginger ale bottle, and a partly filled package of Lucky Strike cigarets, torn at one corner. Mrs. Massie identified the mirror and the package of cigarets as hers.

The officer and his partner said they had found skid marks of automobile tires of a car entering the old quarantine station from the right side of the road. The tire marks appeared to be made by a Silvertown Cord (Goodrich). The officers said they followed the tracks through soft mud to a spot where the grass was flattened alongside a cement slab. That's where they found the articles they brought back. The bottle smelled of liquor.

They said the tire marks indicated that the car had turned around at this point, near the cement slab, and made an exit to Ala Moana Boulevard, turning left and tearing up the dirt as it entered the main road. The officers noted that, while the Silvertown prints on the right side of the car were fairly new, the tread of a Goodyear tire on the right side was worn through.

The detailed statement Thalia Massie made to Captain McIntosh added several new items to the story, although in the main it was the same as her earlier one. She said she had left the party at the Ala Wai Inn about midnight to take a walk and get a breath of fresh air. Describing her abduction, she said her captors put a hand over her mouth and forced her down in the back seat of the car so she wouldn't be visible from the street. She begged them to let her out and offered them money. They asked where the money was. She told them it was in her pocketbook. They searched the pocketbook but found no money.

*The old animal quarantine station was located on the *mauka* side of Ala Moana Boulevard on the Waikiki side of Kewalo Basin.

She said there were at least four men, all Hawaiians. It was obvious from her half-identification of Ida that she had a very hazy idea of what Hawaiians look like, Ida being of Japanese ancestry. She was quite sure one or two of her attackers had raped her more than once. The only names Mrs. Massie said she had heard during the whole episode were Bull, used several times, and some common name like Joe. Asked if she could identify the men if she were to see them again, she answered, "I don't know."

Captain McIntosh asked her about the car and license number. Now, for the first time, she had an answer. She said she thought it was a Ford touring car and the license number was 58–805. She added the number may not be correct because she got only a glimpse of it as they drove away. McIntosh wrote the number down on a blotting pad.

Mrs. Massie said that the boys, before driving away, had told her how to get back on the road. She walked back to the road and hailed a car coming from Waikiki heading toward town. When the people in the car heard she had been assaulted by some Hawaiians, they wanted to take her to the police station. Mrs. Massie insisted she wanted to go to her home in Manoa. They took her there. She told McIntosh she didn't know who the people were, but she was sure they were white. Two men had been in the front seat and two women in the back.

(The day after the story broke in the newspapers, these people came in to police headquarters and gave their evidence. They said Mrs. Massie asked them, "Are you white?" when she hailed their car. They said she told them she thought there were five boys. After leaving Mrs. Massie at her home, they drove back to the spot where they had picked her up. Nearby they found a lady's purse lying by the road. They picked up the purse, brought it along, and gave it to the police. Inside the purse were a lipstick and a powder-puff.)

A short time after Mrs. Massie returned home, her husband telephoned from the Rigby house. She asked him to come home. She said she was dressed at the time in a green dress trimmed with fur. The color of her dress was to prove important in one phase of the case.

That night, another bit of drama held our attention. After hearing Mrs. Massie's story, the captain called in the detective who had arrested Ida and asked the license number of the Ida car. The detective was smart enough not to mention the number in front of Mrs. Massie. Instead, he wrote it down on a piece of paper, holding it so Mrs. Massie couldn't see. The captain pointed to the number Mrs. Massie had given, written on the blotting pad. There was a difference of only one digit between the license number of the Ida car, 58–895, and the number Mrs. Massie said she remembered, 58–805. The number she gave was on the license plate of a truck at Waialua Plantation.

Detectives went to work on Ida. Kalihi and Palama kids don't talk easily to the police. But they will talk like anybody else when police pressure is strong enough. Believe me, it was getting strong that night. Before morning, the detectives had an admission from Ida that he, not some other Japanese boy, had driven the car. He also gave the names of four other young men who rode in the car that night.

Early Sunday morning, police cars rolled up to Kauluwela Park and picked up three young men, like Ida, all in their twenties. They found the fourth the same afternoon and brought him in to headquarters. The youths were unemployed, though some of them in season worked in Honolulu's pineapple canneries. All might be placed among the hundreds of young men who hung around the city's poolrooms for want of employment and for want of anything better to do.

Their names were Joseph Kahahawai, David Takai, Ben Ahakuelo, and Henry Chang. Kahahawai and Ahakuelo were husky Hawaiians, both boxers of sorts. Chang was Chinese and Takai, like Ida, Japanese. Mrs. Homer Peeples was summoned to the station and immediately identified Joseph Kahahawai as the man who had struck her after the near-collision. There was some preliminary questioning.

Early that afternoon, a police inspector and detectives took the four up to the Massie home to see if she could identify them. They found Mrs. Massie being visited by a couple. The inspector went with Mrs. Massie to her bedroom to talk. He said he wanted her to converse with the four suspects to see if she could recognize their voices or anything about them. Mrs. Massie suggested she might remember better in the dark.

If the young men were guilty, what followed must have shaken their nerves a little. The blinds were drawn in the living room and they were lined up. The room was quite dark. Mrs. Massie, her face still swollen and more discolored from the beating than the night before, approached each man and questioned him. The questions in themselves didn't mean much. She asked what their names were and where they had been the night before. All answered they had been at the dance at Waikiki Park.* Mrs. Massie listened intently as they talked. She had regained much of her composure and bore herself well, the detective reported.

The four answered without any noticeable nervousness. She asked Kahahawai if he was called Bull and he answered, "No." She talked to Henry Chang longer than to the others, so it was no surprise to the inspector when, after he had ushered the suspects out, she made a positive identification of him. She also positively identified Joseph Kahahawai. She had no recollection of Takai, but she thought Ida might have been the driver of the car.

Late Sunday evening, with attorneys from City Hall in attendance, Captain McIntosh began taking statements from the five. Their statements pretty well supported one another. Ida had been driving the car around town visiting his friends here and there. Most of the five had drunk a beer or two. Some had visited a *luau* on School Street being given by a mutual friend. Then the carload had headed for a dance at Waikiki Park.

They were remembered at the dance. Some of the girls there remembered Ahakuelo was drunk. One recalled with distaste that he had given her a slap on the seat and that she had refused to dance with him. But another girl did dance with him and she remembered that.

The dance broke up at midnight, just about the time Mrs. Massie said she was leaving the Ala Wai Inn for her breath of fresh air. The five young men loaded into the car and trailed along after a

*Waikiki Park, an amusement center, was located on the Ewa end of where Fort DeRussy is now.

car containing a couple of their friends and two of the girls from the dance. After driving a couple of miles back into Honolulu, the two cars stopped alongside each other. The friends exchanged salutations and then separated again. This was substantiated by the girls and the occupants of the other car.

Shortly after 12:30 A.M., the boys in the Ida car became involved in the incident with Mr. and Mrs. Peeples. This happened in the Palama district on the other side of downtown Honolulu and several miles farther from Waikiki and the scene of the attack. There was no important inconsistency in their stories, and there was no reason to believe any of the witnesses were telling anything but the truth.

Would it be possible for these men to seize the woman, take her to the old animal quarantine station, and rape her six or seven times in no more than twenty minutes? That was about as much time as remained unaccounted for.

On Sunday, too, Captain McIntosh had Ida's car driven to the Massie house to see if she could identify it. She had previously said she believed she would recognize it if she could see the rear seat and the back of the car. It turned out differently when she saw the Ida car. She couldn't identify it then. But in later testimony she stated, "it was just like the car" in which she had been abducted.

Also on Sunday, a U.S. Navy doctor, Lt. Commander John E. Porter, made the first really comprehensive examination of Mrs. Massie and compiled the first complete list of the things that had happened to her physically.

He found a double fracture of the lower jaw so bad that her lower jaw was displaced and would not meet the upper. Some of the teeth on the lower right side were also displaced so that they did not meet the uppers. Three molars on the right side of her jaw were in such proximity to the fracture that they had to be removed ultimately by operation. Both upper and lower lips were swollen and discolored. Her nose was swollen and running from the nasal cavity. The doctor also found small cuts and bruises all over her body. He later explained that Dr. Liu at the Emergency Hospital might not have noticed these, since they became more discolored some hours later. Dr. Porter did not make a vaginal examination but came to the same conclusion as Dr. Liu, that Mrs. Massie might have had intercourse with a number of men without showing any unusual marks or injuries.

The Navy doctor thought her condition so serious that he had her sent to Queen's Hospital late that afternoon. For the next week, the record showed, she ran a temperature of 101 to 104 degrees. Porter called her condition serious throughout that time.

On Monday, an officer took the Ford with license number 58–895 out to the old animal quarantine station. Horace Ida was sent along. Driving beside the tracks discovered previously on the night of the alleged rape, they noted that the tire tracks of Ida's car were identical with the others—three Silvertown cords and one worn Goodyear. The cop said Ida did not deny the similarity.

But the police photographer failed to get pictures of the tire tracks as evidence. When he went to the scene, he took one look and came back without snapping a shutter. In pretty high temper, he explained that the marks of the tires were obliterated. It developed that still another trip had been made to the crime scene. Captain McIntosh and another officer had taken Ida's car out and driven it around the quarantine grounds earlier that day. McIntosh admitted he might have driven over the tracks previously reported, but if so, he did not see them.

On Tuesday morning, a detective took Ida, Kahahawai, and Ahakuelo to Mrs. Massie's room at Queen's Hospital for further questioning. He thought the sight of Mrs. Massie in bed might work on the emotions of the young men enough to make them break down and confess. As a sort of gimmick, the detective put Ida in a chair at the end of the bed facing away from Mrs. Massie. Since she had been held in the back seat, the idea was to simulate the conditions of the ride. After looking Ida over in the chair, she said she thought he might have been the driver.

Also, the detective brought the leather chamois-type jacket Ida had worn. Mrs. Massie had said previously that she remembered a jacket from her struggles during the rape. She felt the jacket to see if she could identify it, then said it felt like the jacket she had touched that night. In earlier questioning, Ida had denied he'd worn the jacket. Later, he admitted he had worn it.

Early that week, too, detectives asked Mrs. Massie again and again whether or not she had heard the license number 58–895 from her husband or from the police radio cars at the emergency hospital. They were trying to clear up the contradiction between her first statement that it had been too dark to see the license plate and her later statement giving the number within one digit. She maintained that she had heard the number from no one, but had merely remembered it.

The local press was beginning to wake up to the fact that Hawaii now had a crime of more than local importance on its hands. The beating and rape of the wife of a naval officer would be front-page news in any circumstance. But the Massies were no ordinary naval couple. Thalia Massie's mother, Mrs. Granville Roland (Grace) Fortescue was a New York and Washington society woman, wife of an author who was distantly related to the late President Theodore Roosevelt. Lieutenant Massie was of a well-to-do Kentucky family. The Massie wedding had been the social event of the year in Washington.

Mrs. Fortescue headed for Hawaii immediately upon getting news of the rape. She rented a house in Manoa. By the time she put in her appearance, the Massie case was the biggest news in Hawaii and it was getting considerable play in mainland newspapers.

In the meantime, police were gathering more evidence, which turned out to be of more use to the defense than the prosecution. For one thing, they found out why Thalia Massie had left the dance at the Ala Wai Inn to get a breath of air. Other naval officers and their wives told detectives there had been a spat between Mrs. Massie and a young officer over a seat.

Thalia had told the officer he was no gentleman. He had retorted by calling her a louse and saying she wasn't wanted around there, anyway. With that, Thalia slapped him in the face. The blow made a sharp crack and caused people to look around. That ended the dispute. Thalia turned around and walked out of the place, apparently to cool herself and her temper in the night air.

The lieutenant's wife said she had stood by not saying a word

73

because she didn't want to get involved. But when she saw Massie later looking for his wife, she told him he'd better find her and take care of her. Thalia Massie was thus presented in a rather unflattering light by those within her own circle, as a woman who wouldn't hesitate to create a scene over a trifle when she'd been drinking. That, of course, didn't mean she hadn't been the victim of a terrible crime.

Then other detectives and I turned up more evidence that the defense eventually used. Three people, two women and a man, came forward to tell how they had been on John Ena Road shortly after midnight on the night of the alleged rape. They had seen a white woman in a green dress, apparently somewhat under the influence of liquor, walking along the street in the direction of Ala Moana. A short distance behind her walked a white man. The man was wearing a dark suit and appeared to be looking at the woman's back.

None of these three witnesses saw a car following anywhere around. But their attention was enough attracted that they watched until the pair went out of sight down the street. The view was cut off there by a curve of the street that went around buildings.

Attorneys presented witnesses and a case to the grand jury on October 12, and Horace Ida, Joseph Kahahawai, Ben Ahakuelo, Henry Chang, and David Takai were all indicted on a charge of rape. The next day, Mrs. Massie was taken to Kapiolani Maternity and Gynecological Hospital because she had missed a menstrual period and feared she was pregnant as a result of the rape. A curettage was performed by her physician. The results showed no sign of pregnancy.

Shortly after that, I came as close to finding eyewitnesses to the crime as I think we ever got. Late one morning in October, going off night duty, I stopped for a cup of coffee at the old Green Mill restaurant on Bethel Street. There I ran into a friend of mine. We sat chewing the fat for a few minutes. He asked me how we were doing on the Massie case.

"Do you think they've got the right boys?" he asked.

"I don't know, Tony," I answered.

"Well, I do, and I'll tell you why."

Then he described a conversation he'd had only a few days after the attack with a Hawaiian from the Big Island. This man told him he'd been riding around that night in a car with a couple of friends. They had seen a gang of boys pulling a woman into a car on John Ena Road at approximately the time the abduction had occurred.

"He knew what he was talking about, too," Tony went on. "The make of the car hadn't been published then in the paper but he knew it. I think he whispered the license number to me, the same one that later came out in the papers."

Well, here was something. I knew the Hawaiian slightly, and Tony gave me the names of the other two men riding with him that night. The next day I dropped a note on the captain's desk. A little later, I was assigned to go out and question the four.

But the Hawaiian didn't tell me the same story that my friend Tony had heard from him, and that the other two told. The latter said they had seen two men, who seemed to be arguing with a *haole* woman on the sidewalk, grab her and drag her into a car that had other men in it. The watchers said they asked their driver, a Filipino, to go slow so they could see what was happening. The car with the woman in the back seat started up and drove off, and that was all they saw.

The Hawaiian had a completely different story. He said two women had called to him from another car and he had turned to look at them. He had asked the driver to slow down so he could see who they were, but he never did recognize them. He had not, the Hawaiian said, seen anybody pull any woman into a car and he had not told my friend Tony that the police had arrested the right gang. Certainly, he insisted, he had not mentioned the make of the car and positively he had mentioned no license number. What he had told Tony, he maintained, was that if the boys in custody had really committed the crime it was a good thing they had been caught.

Tony and the Hawaiian were brought in by attorneys and put

face-to-face to tell their stories. Tony told the same story he had told me and the Hawaiian stuck to his story. So there wasn't much more to do about that.

The case went to trial on November 16 after the usual legal skirmishes by the defense. Feelings were running high. The prosecutor's office had made a number of attempts to get eminent local attorneys to assist with its case, but with no success. The city was divided into two camps—those who believed the boys were guilty, and those who thought they were being framed in some sort of cover-up or that Mrs. Massie wasn't telling the truth.

The latter faction was quick to pick up and spread any rumor that might tend to prove the five local boys innocent. A favorite was that Thalia Massie had really been beaten and raped by a Navy officer. There were all sorts of variations on this theme, most of them casting libelous aspersions on the reputations of the naval personnel concerned. In all truth, I had to admit there were policemen who contributed as much to such rumors as anyone. On the other hand, from the talk of some of the admirals and Navy brass you might have gotten the idea that the trial should be a mere formality preceding perhaps a hanging.

There was also the matter of race. In Hawaii, the melting pot of the Pacific, race relations were far better than in most places on the mainland. Still, friction did exist between "local" people and *haoles*. This was fanned into something much bigger by all the publicity and the rumor-spreading.

Griffin Wight, Deputy City and County Attorney, was in charge of the prosecution while William Heen, one of the best local defense lawyers, represented the five accused. The star witness, of course, was Thalia Massie. In many ways she was not as satisfactory a witness as the prosecution might have hoped. She gave a clear enough account of her abduction, assault, and the rape itself, but she was very hazy on the manner in which she had identified her assailants later. Also, she failed to remember statements she had made that were a matter of police record, with more than one witness testifying to them.

The young woman had excellent reasons for being hazy, of course. As she said, she had been suffering from shock the first

76

time she was asked to identify any suspects. Later, she had been shot full of sedatives. But she remembered so many more things at the trial than she had ever told police that Mr. Heen was afforded many openings for cross-examination that helped cast doubt on her credibility. Maybe, in view of her early statements, her testimony of what happened was too clear. Mr. Heen did not fail to point out that Thalia Massie's memory seemed to be getting better the farther the night of September 12 receded into the past.

When he came to his argument, Mr. Heen was able to put many doubts in the minds of the jurors. Thalia Massie's clothes had been introduced into evidence and they showed little sign of rough handling. The skillful defense attorney had much to say about that. Then there was the woman in the green dress who had been seen by three witnesses, the woman who had been followed by a single Caucasian man close behind. Mrs. Massie had been wearing a green dress. Might not this have been Mrs. Massie and might not this man have beaten her up? Might not this have been some acquaintance? Might not she have been beaten up as a result of some lovers' quarrel? After all, who was there to say a rape ever actually happened at all? Did any doctor who examined Mrs. Massie ever find positive signs of rape?

Woven well into the fabric of his speech, though never introduced outright, was the thought that the man behind the woman in the green dress might well have been the lieutenant who had been arrested with his fly open, up in Manoa later. Lieutenant Archer, ever destined to be unlucky, was the obvious suspect. The implication, clear though not specifically stated, was that this *haole* woman, in order to throw the blame away from her own *haole* lover, had made up a story about a gang of local boys. When this particular group had been arrested, she had been at first bewildered, then determined to hang it on them to establish her own story more firmly.

I asked Wight again and again to bring in Archer as a witness and have him testify. Archer could have established clearly his presence in various places, creating an unbreakable alibi for himself and robbing the defense of that alternative. But I was not able to convince the county attorney.

Now, as it happened, a break came in the case. It concerned the woman in the green dress. Outside in the corridor, during a recess, an acquaintance approached me. He had heard Mr. Heen's argument about the white man following the white woman in the green dress, and he had the answer to that one. He knew the woman in the green dress. He knew that the man behind her that night was no naval lieutenant because he was her husband. He told me the woman's name and said she was a patient at the moment in Tripler General Hospital.

In no time at all, I was in the courtroom where I told the bailiff I wanted to see Mr. Wight outside. In the corridor, I described what I had heard. He went back in and asked for a recess. Soon I was in Judge Alva Steadman's chambers telling the story to the judge and attorneys for the prosecution and defense. The judge wanted to know the name of my informant and I refused to give it.

But the next morning he re-opened the case to allow the new witnesses to testify. The attorneys and court reporter went to Tripler Hospital to get the ailing woman's deposition. It turned out to be just as my informant had said. She said she was the woman in the green dress and the man behind her had been her husband; he came in and testified in corroboration of his wife's deposition. However, Mr. Heen brought forward two witnesses who refuted this testimony, saying they knew the woman and her husband and that they were not on the scene.

The jury deliberated ninety-seven hours, then failed to agree. They were divided six to six. Judge Steadman declared a mistrial on December 6.

Now began the really sensational part of the case, though I had no part in it, having been assigned to chasing a Filipino killer. The hung jury and mistrial aroused the Navy to strong feelings against local boys. Six days after the mistrial was declared, a gang of Navy men took Horace Ida out to the cliff we call the Pali, beat him up and threatened to throw him over unless he confessed to guilt in the rape case. So far as I heard, he did not confess.

A little less than a month after that, on January 8, Lieutenant Massie, Mrs. Fortescue, and two naval enlisted men abducted Joseph Kahahawai from in front of the Judiciary Building and took him to the Massie home in Manoa. There Massie killed him with a Navy pistol. Three of them were apprehended on the way to the Koko Head Blow Hole, one of Oahu's famous scenic spots, where they intended to dispose of the body by throwing it into the Blow Hole, in the belief that it would be carried out to sea.

Another false rumor that spread after the murder of Kahahawai was that the socially prominent Mrs. Fortescue had ordered him castrated after death. This was absolutely untrue. I saw pictures of Kahahawai's body taken at the city morgue and read the autopsy report. There was no such mutilation.

The trial that followed was a sensation, and the story appeared on front pages all over the country. Clarence Darrow, the great defense attorney, was lured out of retirement to represent the Massies. He did a masterful job. But he was faced with an able opponent, John Kelley, who had become prosecutor in the meantime. What might have been a case of second-degree murder was reduced by the jury to manslaughter. The judge sentenced the four involved to ten years in prison each. Within an hour (an hour which all of them spent pleasantly in the governor's office), Governor Lawrence Judd issued a commutation of sentence and all four went free.*

Four days later, the Massies, Mrs. Fortescue, and Mr. Darrow boarded a ship for the mainland. John Kelley wasn't quite

---

*Governor Judd had been under intense pressure to free the defendants. Following the guilty verdict, the Hearst newspaper chain in all editions ran a front page box imploring readers to "Write Your Representatives in Washington to Take the Necessary Steps to Protect the Honor of American Womanhood in the American Possession of Hawaii, and Also to Compel Decent Respect on the Part of the Hawaiian Rabble for Our American Nation and Our Nation's Patriotic Defenders" (Peter Van Slingerland, *Something Terrible Has Happened* [New York: Harper & Row, 1966], 283). Representative Fred A. Britton of Illinois, ranking Republican member of the House Naval Affairs Committee, stated: "The duty of our Government now is to see that law and order are maintained in Hawaii, even if it becomes necessary to establish military rule." The General Assembly of Kentucky passed a resolution urging "every arm of the government to be called into use to ensure immediate release of the four defendants and that President Hoover declare martial law in Honolulu until such time as Hawaii can be made safe for women" (Peter Packer and Bob Thomas, *The Massie Case* [New York: Bantam Books, 1966], ii). "Governor Judd was instructed by Washington to commute their sentences [of Thomas Massie and Mrs. Fortescue] within one day of their conviction" (Lawrence H. Fuchs, *Hawaii Pono, A Social History* [New York: Harcourt, Brace & World, 1961], 189).

through. Having every intention of trying the local boys again for the crime of rape, he issued a subpoena for Mrs. Massie. She stayed behind the bolted door of her stateroom until the ship sailed, and so the subpoena could not be served. Later, on the West Coast, she told reporters she had dodged because she did not want to go through another trial. She said she didn't think it would accomplish anything, that the local boys would never be found guilty by a local jury.

There was nothing to justify Thalia Massie's statement. I for one believe John Kelley would have given the case the same vigorous prosecution he gave every other case the grand jury sent him. But he had gone as far as anyone could reasonably expect him to.

With the principal witness on the mainland and unwilling to back up her complaint, Kelley asked for a writ of nolle prosequi, citing other reasons it would be difficult, if not impossible, to get a conviction. He pointed out that the medical evidence to substantiate the rape charge was not conclusive, that the five men charged had an alibi which no evidence yet had seriously damaged, and that the identification of them and their car had been done in a prejudicial manner both by the complaining witness and the police in a way that left the result far from conclusive.

Kelley reminded the court that the attorney general had made as careful an investigation as possible and that the Pinkerton Detective Agency had been called in to make an investigation. Neither had brought forward evidence that would strengthen the prosecution's case. As a result, there was no more likelihood now that a conviction could be obtained in a retrial. The writ was granted.

To this day, though reams have been written about the case, nothing more of tangible, material evidence has been discovered. The most important questions still asked have never been satisfactorily answered. Most especially, were the five accused men guilty?

The jury that tried them were divided evenly on the question and a mistrial was declared. Opinion among people in all walks of life in Honolulu was divided almost as evenly. There have been some highly credible sounding stories about another gang roving the town that night who might have been guilty instead of the five who were tried and whose alibis seemed very strong. I do not reject that possibility. But the stories have not led to any tangible evidence. The solution of this crime will be established now only through a confession by some individual who helped commit it.

Then there's another question that keeps recurring: might not Lieutenant Archer of the Navy, the man with a whiskey breath and his fly open, have abducted, beat up, and assaulted Mrs. Massie? My answer is merely that there was not a bit of evidence pointing in that direction. There was considerable evidence to support the lieutenant's story and it was corroborated by Thomas Massie. To my mind, the continued repetition of stories about "that Navy lieutenant" is absurd.

One thing there is no question about, the Massie case hit Hawaii hard. I won't be surprised one of these days when some history student brings out a study to show how many years the Massie case held back Hawaiian Statehood.* If you believed the picture drawn in mainland magazines, you viewed Hawaii as a place where half-savage natives and Orientals waited around slavering to find a white woman they could drag off into the jungle and rape. The local law, in that picture, was a farce and police and prosecutors something akin to Keystone Comedy cops.

One result of all this was high sensitivity on the part of tourist agents, Chamber of Commerce officials, and other citizens to unfavorable publicity about Hawaii. A newsman has told the story of being stopped by one of these nervous souls while he was hurrying down the street on December 7, 1941, to get off stories about the bombing of Pearl Harbor.

"I suppose you're going to blow this thing out of all proportion," said the concerned citizen caustically.

---

*Theon Wright, in his forward to *Rape in Paradise* (New York: Hawthorne Books, Inc.), published eight years after Jardine completed his manuscript with Ed Rohrbough, wrote: "This case almost ended self-government in Hawaii. For twenty years it delayed Hawaii's entry into the Federal Union as a state. . . ."

9

How I "Made" Sergeant

When a storm as big as the Massie case blows up, heads invariably topple regardless of whether or not they're the right heads. The police force was taken away from control by the City and County government and put under a commission appointed by the Governor of Hawaii.* That meant the end of Sheriff Pat Gleason as boss of the police.

Many of us regretted it. Pat Gleason was a conscientious official and a hard worker. The rate of crime detection and the proportion of arrests and convictions under him were, I believe, just as good as they were under other police heads at different periods in Honolulu.

The new commission, eager to justify its existence, brought in Charles F. Weeber, formerly of the U.S. Army, to head the department. It also brought in William A. Gabrielson of the Berkeley, California, police department, on loan to help implement the reorganization. Gabrielson was responsible for the motorization of our police, the systematizing of our Records Division, the restyling of uniforms and badges, and the shifting about of personnel.

Weeber, a strict disciplinarian and good organizer, though with

*The Honolulu Police Department, A Brief History, by Leon Straus, published in 1978, explains that backlash from the Massie case created demands for a change in police organization. During this period, two convicts escaped from Oahu Prison. One of them burglarized the home of a business executive and raped his wife. Meanwhile, Assistant United States Attorney Seth Richardson arrived from Washington to make an in-depth survey of conditions in the islands. His findings were favorable except for laxity in law enforcement. Governor Judd called the Territorial legislature into session in January 1932. A bill was passed and signed into law designed to remove police work from politics. The law eliminated the office of elected sheriff and replaced it with the chief of police, an appointment made by a five-member police commission appointed by the governor. Another new law created the office of City and County Public Prosecutor to handle all criminal matters, the prosecutor to be appointed by the mayor, not elected.

no real experience in police work, took the top job with the understanding he would remain only six months. At the end of that time, he resigned and took a position with the wealthy Dillingham interests. Gabrielson, instead of returning to Berkeley, stayed on to become chief of police on August 8, 1932.

Other effects of the Massie case and the subsequent coming of Weeber and Gabrielson and modernization of the Honolulu Police Department included all sorts of efforts at training and retraining us. Most of the innovations were good and, I suppose, inevitable. But there were some that bordered on the ridiculous and others exasperated us. We had an instructor who gave us lectures on police theory. He was no more of a theoretician than we were. Everything he knew came out of a book he kept open before him and to which he referred constantly during his lectures.

"I could do just as well," Bill Clark, one of the cops, told me one night. "In fact, I could do better because I'd just read from the book. This guy goes out on his own a little to try and sound like an expert. The chances are that that part is all wrong."

"Maybe he knows more than you think," I said, kidding Bill along.

"You watch," he said. "I'll prove it to you."

The next time we assembled for a lecture, the instructor appeared with a worried look on his face. He announced there wouldn't be any lecture that night. When we got outside, Bill Clark chortled and said, "I told you! I told you!" He had swiped the instructor's book and hidden it. Without that book, the teacher was nowhere.

Another training course we had was police judo. For this we reported to the armory where mats were laid out. The teacher taught holds, disarming a criminal, stuff like that. The irony of the whole thing was that there were hundreds of Japanese in Honolulu who knew more judo than we'd ever know. The teacher was a mainland *haole* who'd learned a couple of holds somewhere and figured he was pretty good. There were even men on the force who could take his measure.

He got away with it for awhile. Finally, a big Hawaiian cop who had learned a little judo around town picked up teacher and slammed him down on the mat. Teacher almost had his back broken and was laid up for several days. He never got around to resuming the police judo classes. The project was gradually forgotten.

This doesn't mean the department didn't need a little stiffening. Over a period of years, some of us on the force had come to have a somewhat careless attitude about one offense that was, in Gabrielson's eyes, the worst possible crime for a policeman. That was being under the influence of liquor while on duty. Certainly we had developed the habit of covering up for one another.

I remember, some time after Gabrielson became chief, when I turned out the watch in the Detective Division one Sunday night in holiday season and every stinking son on the watch showed up pie-eyed. I was the only sober man in the room. What was I going to do? When the calls started coming in, was I going to send out a bunch of drunken detectives? Or was I going to report the whole watch to the chief?

I decided that, no matter what happened, I wasn't turning in reports on my fellow officers even though I, as lieutenant, was responsible for them. I chewed them out and told them to go home. If anyone called, they were to explain they were sick. Then I took a seat by the telephone and got ready to be a one-man detective division.

We were lucky. As it happened, not a single call came in for detectives that night. Next night when the boys came on duty they were penitent and very grateful. They knew what would have happened to me if anyone had found out my whole command had gone home "sick" and I hadn't even reported it to the chief.

Then I got myself in trouble. After working most of the night on a case, I went through one of those judo sessions at the armory late next morning. The tension of work and training was getting to me, and the idea of a drink at the time seemed just right. A friend and I went out and had a few. The first drink seemed only an invitation to another, and another, and so on. I knew I should have eaten lunch and had a couple hours of rest before going on duty. But I didn't.

The result was that, when I reported for duty at four o'clock in the afternoon, I was pretty close to being plastered. A detective, a fair-weather friend who may have been looking for my job, sent word to the chief's office that I was down there drunk. Technically, he did his duty. But it was a duty that had been observed more in the omission than in the execution. I can't bring myself to respect the man to this day.

The first thing I knew, Captain Griffin and Chief Gabrielson came charging in on me. They got a couple of whiffs of my breath and ordered a car to take me to the emergency hospital and give me a sobriety test. It was the same one given drivers caught smelling like that behind steering wheels.

I didn't say much until we got there. But with a charge of drunkenness closing in on me, I turned loose on them, insisting that I was a victim of injustice. Here I was working night and day and making a lot of good arrests, only to get hauled up the first time I came around with a little too much liquor in me. It made me more angry telling them about it. I called them every foul name I could think of, aiming most of it at Gabrielson, piling up more charges against myself. Griffin sat there calmly writing down what I said as if he were taking the confession of a criminal. That didn't calm me down at all. Instead, it inspired me to call them a few names I might not have thought of otherwise.

The doctor on duty was a friend of mine. I could see he was doing his best to stall the actual test. Finally, he said he'd have to call Dr. Thomas Mossman, the head county physician, to give the test in a matter as important as this. Dr. Mossman was another friend. He stalled for awhile, too, when he got there. Every time he got in a position where Gabrielson and Griffin couldn't see him, he put his finger to his lips in a sign for me to shut up. I knew he made sense, but I was too angry and reckless at the moment to care. I went right on cussing the chief and sounding, I imagine, pretty much like every other angry drunk that gets taken up for a test.

As it turned out, the test showed a reading of only 2.5, so I couldn't have been so very drunk. But I might as well have been, with the show I'd put on. After we got back to headquarters, I walked into the office of Captain McIntosh, in command of the

Detective Division, and put my badge on his desk along with my handcuffs, book of city ordinances, and rule book. I figured I was through anyway, so I'd get the jump on Chief Gabrielson and quit before he fired me.

Then I went home and stayed there. Four days later, one of the dicks came around to see me. He said he'd been sent by Captain McIntosh to ask me to come back. I refused. I told him I was through and there was no point going back to talk about it. The next day, the same detective returned. He said McIntosh had again asked me to come back. The captain sent word that, even if I wanted to quit, there was nothing to be lost by coming back to talk a little. This time I decided to go. Captain McIntosh grabbed my hand and told me how sorry he was the whole thing had happened. He said he didn't want to lose me from the division.

"You'll have to go in to see the chief, John," he said. "Go ahead. He may break you but don't let it stop you. You'll be back up again. You're too good a detective not to be."

I had my doubts, but McIntosh finally persuaded me to take my badge back. He urged me to stop by Captain Griffin's office before I went to see the chief. Captain Griffin was just as friendly and sympathetic. He told me he had wanted no part of what happened. But he'd been handy when the chief started after me, so Gabrielson had grabbed him to come along as a witness. Griffin encouraged me to go in and see the chief. He wished me good luck.

The session in there was short. I'll never forget it, nor the way Gabrielson looked that day. He expected me to crawl and beg and ask for my job back. Anticipation was written all over him. I just stood there and waited for him to do the talking. He fiddled around a little but I just waited.

"Well, you know I've got to do something," he said finally. "What would you do if you were in my place and I were in yours?"

"I know what I'd do in your place," I told him, "but I'm not in your place, so there's no point in talking about it."

He waited a little longer and then said, "Okay, you're busted. You're reduced to the rank of detective for appearing on duty under the influence of liquor. Give me your badge."

I laid my lieutenant's badge on his desk. The chief slid a detective's badge across the table to me. So I started again to work from the bottom. For a while I had hopes of doing what McIntosh had said, rising back my old rank. I had good luck, too, and cracked some tough cases in the next few months. McIntosh went to the chief to argue that I should be restored to rank. Gabrielson wouldn't do it. He said discipline would suffer if he put me back to lieutenant. However, even he couldn't ignore the work I was doing. So he created this new position of sergeant of detectives. Until then, there hadn't been any rank between detective and lieutenant. I was sergeant for a long time.

10

The Burglar Who Lectured Police

THERE is no doubt that Chief Gabrielson had a big impact on the Honolulu Police Department, but the way he went about it didn't always win him a lot of friends on the force. That doesn't mean he wasn't a highly efficient police officer. Anyway, here's an example.

About a year after he took over, a gang of burglars pulled a string of jobs that had the police, as the newspapers love to say, "baffled." We thought most of the jobs were being pulled by the same operators. But there wasn't a pattern. The burglars hit a big grocery store and a plumbing company, then a couple of furniture outlets and a wholesale dairy firm. Next they took the offices of a prominent physician, a soft-drink stand, a restaurant, and a drug store.

Detective John R. Troche and I were assigned to most of the major burglaries, so we felt the heat. We began a drive on July 20, 1933, to clean up our cases. Six days later we arrested three suspects in connection with the theft of fifteen cases of tobacco from the warehouse of the Western States Grocery on Punchbowl Street. This trio had done time in the Territorial penitentiary. It didn't take us long to figure out who the brains of the outfit was—a young Spaniard named Joseph Rogelio from Barcelona.

He considered himself an artist and took as much pride in burglary as a matador does in killing a bull. By playing to his enormous ego, we soon had him boasting of the jobs he had engineered and executed right under our noses. He confessed to all the major burglaries we were working on in addition to the Western States Grocery job. Both Troche and I were tired when we returned Rogelio to his cell in the police station lockup early that afternoon, but we glowed with the satisfaction that we had wrapped up the baffling burglaries.

Half an hour later, we walked by the patrol squad room on our way out of police headquarters when an unusual spectacle stopped us at the door. Sixty patrolmen were lined up at attention in preparation for their tour of duty. Before them stood Chief William A. Gabrielson and the man who had been boasting to us all morning, Joseph Rogelio, the burglar.

Something about the whole set-up just held us there. Far from looking guilty, Rogelio was swaggering around as if he were running the show. Gabrielson explained to the officers that he had asked Rogelio, a "good burglar," to give the police a lesson in crime that he hoped might do them some good. Then he told Rogelio to give his lecture and to "go as far as you like." Before we were over the surprise of seeing this criminal on such easy terms with the chief, Rogelio was letting the cops have it.

"You're all dumbbells," he told them as he walked up the aisle, every eye focused on him. "You're too dumb to use your heads." They winced. "Now I'm going to tell you how dumb you really are, before they send me up."

From there on the lecture got worse, at least from a policeman's point of view. Rogelio was unrepentant, uncowed, and uninhibited. He was a double-barreled, revolving cop-hater, and he was having the time of his life. If I live to be a hundred, I shall never forget the sight of his stocky body swaggering up and down in front of the line of policemen in the squad room, the sneer on his swarthy face, and the scorn in his loud, rasping voice. It hurt worse to know that what he said wasn't all braggadocio. Rogelio was telling the truth as he had been telling it to us all morning.

"I want you guys to know how I ran rings around you before you got me on the Western States Grocery job," he sneered. "You had plenty of chances to get me, but you always messed up. Take the time I swiped those cigaret machines from the Blue Bird Cafe last month. One of you guys, I don't know who, got suspicious and stopped me just after I pulled the job. But he didn't look in the back of my truck where the cigaret machines were. Another time you could have caught me easy during a break-in. The officer on the beat came along and tried the door and never guessed I was hanging on the other side."

The policemen glared at him. They would have been happy to string him up in the squad room, but the burglar went right on. He knew he had a captive audience.

"You birds were asleep the time I pulled the job at Dr. Fronk's office," he said. "I climbed the drainpipe leading to his office four or five times that night. The first time, I found the door locked and had to go back for my tools. Then I had to make a couple of other trips up and down, bringing out the stuff we stole. My pal stood watch at the bottom of the pipe."

Ignoring the hard breathing that had developed among his listeners, Rogelio went on to the next part of his lesson.

"You guys are a bunch of fish. Do you want to know how I pulled the Western States Grocery job? Well, I'll tell you. Me and my partner watched the man on the beat for more than a week and found out exactly what time he passed the place. It was 2:10 A.M. Then he wouldn't come by for another hour. Every night it was the same. At 2:15 we crashed the place and about 3 o'clock we dunked the lights and laid low for about fifteen minutes. The cop never got wise."

Rogelio continued with the attitude of one who wishes to give the devil his due.

"But I have to hand it to you guys a little bit. You were on the job a couple of times. Once me and my partner were coming in from Kaneohe intending to pull a job, when a cop smelled a rat and started to follow us. He hung on our tail until we finally got leary and went home."

Summing up his critique, Rogelio added, "The trouble with most of you cops is you ain't suspicious enough. When you see a couple of us jailbirds together, you ought to suspect something is up. But you only bring us to the station for investigation and then let us go. I'll say one thing, though. You've improved since I first went to jail."

Then, to add insult to injury, he explained that he had confessed out of the goodness of his heart: "The detectives were very nice. They treated me like a gentleman. If they'd been tough, I'd never have told them anything. It makes a lot of difference the way you're treated. I got nothing but praise for the way the detectives handled me after I was picked up."

A couple of reporters from the *Star-Bulletin* and *The Advertiser* were standing there. I knew Chief Gabrielson had invited them in for the show. He stepped up himself, grinning like a Cheshire cat, and made a short, polite speech of thanks to Rogelio.

"That talk did more to help our officers than weeks of lecturing," he said. "The men will undoubtedly take the cue and be better officers for it. Rogelio's remark that you men are not sufficiently suspicious is especially valuable. The best officer is a suspicious officer. Officers in Honolulu are likely to become careless because there are so few smart burglars here. Rogelio's talk will snap them out of it."

Well, that really burned us up. Nor had we heard the last of Rogelio's talk. The same day a circular was issued from the chief's office calling the attention of all officers to a regulation which required that they follow no set rule in making their rounds and that they go through alleyways, lanes, and areaways in checking their beats. The next day, the story was in the newspapers. Cops were kidded all over town. I was happy to be a plainclothes detective, because the uniformed police were all being called dumbbells.

But Rogelio didn't get the last laugh. Three days later he took his turn as listener while Judge Albert M. Cristy in Circuit Court told him in plain language who was the dumbbell.

"You may have a poor opinion of the ability of the Police Department to find the fellow who is trying to beat them," said Cristy. "You may beat them twenty-five or fifty times. But sooner or later the question of who is the 'dumbbell' is answered. You are the one who is up against it now, not the Police Department. When I put you on probation, I thought I saw in you the ability to handle liberty if you were given a chance. But you could not use it."

It was quite a long lecture. After he finished, Judge Cristy gave the city police mentor thirty-three years in the penitentiary.

It may seem naive of me to become exercised because a punk

91

like Rogelio called the cops dumbbells, but I can't help it. At the same time he was being sentenced, across the street in Iolani Palace eight veteran police officers were being congratulated by the governor of the Territory on their retirement. Those dumbbells had done their duty honorably and were going on pension while Rogelio was going to jail. Which was the smartest?

11

Murder Won't Burn

AT about eight o'clock on a September morning in 1933, an underworld source gave Detective Troche and me a strange tip. It was to the effect that one Francisco Lopez, also known as Francisco Mangual, a paroled convict, had disappeared three or four years earlier as a result of foul play. Neither of us knew anything at the time about Francisco Lopez. Apparently, to the police he had never amounted to much. The disappearance of a convict had not aroused the community. But a policeman does not solve crimes committed only against people of good reputation. We immediately began checking. The trail led us to the most cold-blooded killer I have ever known.

It was a shadowy trail at first. The records showed that Francisco Lopez had been paroled from Oahu Prison in 1924. He had reported to his parole officer for three months. Since then, the record was blank, although there was plenty before that. From 1901 to 1920 he had been in prison for charges ranging from affray to grand larceny. At the time of his parole, he had done four years of a five-to-twenty stretch for burglary.

A check at the Bureau of Vital Statistics proved just as unenlightening. There was no record of Lopez' death. If he was dead. We communicated with police departments on the neighbor islands for information about him. There was nothing. No hard evidence that a crime had been committed. Just that tip. But what had happened to Lopez?

We asked around and discovered he had two brothers who lived in Honolulu on Auld Lane in the Palama section. One brother told us he had last seen Francisco nine years earlier, on Maui. Later, in

Honolulu, he had asked acquaintances about his brother and was told he had disappeared under suspicious circumstances.

I had learned long ago that many members of the Puerto Rican community buttoned their lips when police came asking questions. But Troche and I had an advantage, he being of Puerto Rican ancestry and I being Portuguese, which is considered like a first cousin of the Puerto Rican. We pursued our sources to find that Lopez had once lived for a time in a shack in Field 11, Aiea Plantation, with another Puerto Rican named Felix Flores, now a convict serving time at the Waiakea Prison Camp on the Big Island on a conviction of assault with a deadly weapon.

Then we heard that Lopez had some friends named Mr. and Mrs. Bautista Bales who lived at Red Hill in Honolulu. We drove out to interview them. The couple confirmed that Lopez and Flores had lived together in the plantation shack and that they had come occasionally to visit at the Bales' home. But neither Bautista Bales nor his wife had seen Francisco since 1930. When Flores had come to visit alone, they asked him about Lopez. Flores answered that Lopez had left, and he didn't know where he could be found.

We took the information we had collected to Captain McIntosh, chief of detectives, and asked to have the prison bring Flores from Hawaii Island to Honolulu for questioning. He arrived eight days later, a stocky man with gray edging into his black hair, though not into his mustache. He had cold black eyes and, we were to discover, as cold a heart inside him as a man ever had.

At police headquarters we put him under questioning in Spanish. Troche understood him better than I. Flores gave out the vital statistics readily enough: fifty-six years old, born in Puerto Rico, arrived in Hawaii thirty-three years before. He told of the conviction under which he was then in prison. But when we asked him about Lopez, he would only shake his head and reply, "Yo no se" ("I don't know").

The next morning we were at him again. Both Troche and I had developed questioning techniques to make prisoners talk. We tried everything we knew with no success. He was a very tough nut to crack. We had just about given up when Flores shrugged his shoulders and admitted it. He said he had killed Lopez but that it wasn't murder. There had been a fight and he had won, that's all. Between two men like that, a fight could only end in death of the loser.

Once a killer decides to confess, he will often talk your ear off because it's a relief to get it off his chest after holding back for so long. Flores was like that. He talked for almost an hour in monotonous, unemotional Spanish, telling us the bloodiest story we had ever heard.

He said he and Lopez had been friends when they lived in the shack in Field 11 of Aiea Plantation where, Flores said, he raised vegetables. He said a tension developed between them because Lopez was jealous of his success with vegetables. Or maybe the jealousy was merely a sign of the tension. There were arguments about small matters. Sometimes Lopez would threaten him. Flores said he believed his friend was capable of violence because he had heard dark stories of the other man's past.

On April 15, 1930, the argument got hotter. Flores said he accused Lopez of being a murderer as well as the thief he had been proved to be before being sent to prison. At that, Lopez grabbed a cane knife and made three swings at him. Ducking and dodging with agility, Flores ran into the shack to get his own cane knife. He rushed back out to find Lopez still after him. He swung a powerful blow that cut off Lopez' arm at the shoulder. Lopez fell to the ground. Before he could cry out, Flores cut off his head with another swing.

"But," I asked in my Portuguese-style Spanish, "didn't this bother your conscience?"

"Porque?" ("Why should it?") answered the convict without a trace of facial expression. Then he added in Spanish, "If it were to happen the same way again, I would kill him again."

With blood in pools on the ground and the body of his former friend lying decapitated before him, Flores set about removing the signs of the crime. He hadn't much fear of discovery. The shack was five miles back from the highway. Visitors seldom showed up there.

The killer cleaned himself thoroughly, changed clothes, and walked into Aiea where he bought five gallons of kerosene. Then he returned and made preparations to dispose of the body. He dug a shallow pit, rolled the body in, and covered it with branches cut from a mango tree nearby. He soaked the whole thing with kerosene and set it afire.

By the time the fire burned out, he discovered that it is harder to get rid of a human body than he'd anticipated. Again and again he would burn out a set of branches, only to find Lopez' body pretty much intact. For five days and nights he tended the gruesome pyre, watching the black smoke roll into the blue Hawaiian sky, while the body slowly disintegrated.

The flesh was all burned away from the bones at the end of the fifth day. Flores dug another pit at the foot of the mango tree and carefully assembled the bones in the pit so they would look like a natural skeleton. After filling in the shallow grave, a foot and a half below the jungle grass, he took his leave of the place. He told us he went to the home of his daughter in Watertown* and stayed about a month before leaving Honolulu for the island of Kauai.

When Flores had finished his story, he led a grim procession of policemen and detectives to the cane field at Aiea Plantation. Without hesitation, he pointed out the mango tree that served as a marker for the grave. Our men dug where Flores directed. Within a short time they unearthed the bones as he had described them.

The killer seemed unaffected by the sight of the bones. He got down into the grave and helped pick out the fragments and put them in a box we had brought for the purpose. Among the bone fragments we found a silver ring that showed evidence of having been subjected to intense heat. Flores said the ring had belonged to Lopez. Then the killer posed for a police photograph with the box of bones, as if it were a trophy he had won at bowling.

Back at the police station, Troche and I set about checking his confession. We discovered that Flores' story dove-tailed exactly with every check that could be established. The Hawaiian Criminological Laboratory found that the fragments were all human as claimed, that they were bones of only one body, and that they were those of an adult male. Lonisio Lopez, brother of the dead man,

*Watertown was a small community located *makai* of the present Honolulu International Airport.

looked at the ring and said it was similar to a ring his brother had worn. But he could not make a positive identification because the setting had been melted and disfigured beyond recognition.

Then we began finding new witnesses to establish more evidence for a charge of murder. A man came forward to tell us he had visited a shack in Field 11 to find a fire burning in the front yard and Felix Flores up in the mango tree cutting branches. When Flores came down, he told this witness in Spanish, "There's the son of a bitch. I killed him and I'm burning his body now." The witness said he didn't wait around long enough to look into the fire, but there was no doubt he was thoroughly impressed.

The same witness said Flores had visited him at his home on Desha Lane in Honolulu that same night and had told him he was going to Kauai because he had killed Mangual, the name by which Lopez was known. Another witness, who had been present in the home on Desha Lane when the conversation took place, confirmed this statement.

One witness led to another. A woman from the camp of Puerto Rican workers at Aiea told us she had been doing laundry for Lopez. One day Flores came to her home saying he had been sent to pick up Lopez' laundry and that they were both going to Kauai. He took away two suitcases full of clothes.

Then Troche and I interviewed the daughter of Flores who had been living in Watertown at the time Lopez disappeared. She recalled that her father had stopped at the house and stayed about a month with her and her husband. When she told her father that he looked sick and run-down, he answered that he had killed a man with a knife and that he was going to Kauai. But he didn't say who the man was.

Another trip to the Bales' home gave us a much more complete story than we had heard the first time. They said Flores had not only stopped at their house but had stayed overnight. About 1 A.M. Mrs. Bales was awakened by Flores shouting as if he were having a nightmare. She said he was being bothered by a spirit. She heard him cry out for someone to "get the hell out of here. If you bother me, I will kill you."

After swearing and using violent language for some time, Mrs.

Bales said, Flores went outside to pick some branches of a plant called *ruda,* held sacred by Puerto Ricans. He brought the branches back into his room and waved them over his body to frighten away the spirit that was bothering him. Mrs. Bales said Flores quieted down after awhile, then seemed to realize he had an audience. He pounded on the wall of his room and shouted, "If anyone gives me away, I will come back and kill them and burn this house."

The unruly guest made his departure the next morning. Mrs. Bales said she had her daughter write the date and put it in a trunk because she thought something might come of all this later. After telling us this, she went to her trunk, opened it and brought out a piece of paper with the words, "July 4, 1930," written on it. The husband now told us Flores had confessed the killing to him in much the same detail as we had already heard it. But Bales had been too afraid of Flores' vengeance to tell police.

Well, Troche and I had cleared up a three-year-old murder. Then Flores started us after a couple of other murders, much older. He said Lopez had killed a Puerto Rican named Ramon de Leon at the village of Kukuihaele on Hawaii Island, about twenty years before. Lopez had described how he struck de Leon in the back of the head with a stick. He robbed him of twenty-five or thirty dollars and threw his body into a pond near the highway. The victim had been carrying a lantern and a bag of corn. Then there was a Japanese man, whose name Flores didn't recall, on Kauai whom Lopez had admitted murdering ten years before. According to Flores, Lopez told him he'd been burglarizing a house when the Japanese surprised him. So he killed the Japanese.

We went to work again. This time we found a witness who remembered the facts of de Leon's death about as Flores described them. The lantern and the bag of corn had been found along the road. And de Leon's body had been found in the pond. The indications were that he had received a blow on the head. The stick was found along the road, too, but no one had ever been arrested for the crime. We uncovered nothing more on either murder. It occurred to us, of course, that Flores might be trying to unload old crimes of his own on the dead Lopez.

Our evidence resulted in an indictment on November 9, 1933, of Felix Flores for murder in the second degree. But, though he freely confessed to killing Lopez, he pleaded not guilty by reason of self-defense. Deputy Public Prosecutor Edward N. Sylva eventually had to agree with him. Sylva pointed out to the court, in moving for a nolle prosequi of the case, that there were no witnesses to dispute the killer's claim. So Flores went back to his cell to finish serving his time on the old conviction of assault with a deadly weapon. There was nothing Troche and I could do about it. We knew he had killed one man, maybe three, and perhaps more we didn't know about. But, though we had solved our case to the satisfaction of everyone, the law was powerless to punish him.

12

A Lucid Interval of Murder

T HE job of a police detective is a lot less glamorous than many people think. Most often the big break in a case comes not from detecting at all, but through a tip from some down-at-the-heel stool pigeon no respectable citizen cares to associate with. That's why I regularly visited Oahu Prison and gave inmates a few dollars from my own pocket to buy cigarets and candy at the prison canteen. There was no fund for this sort of thing, but those investments paid off in information I couldn't have gotten any other way.

Much of the effort I put into investigating crimes wasn't even directed at finding out who did them. We already knew that. The problem was to build a case so airtight no clever defense attorney could find a loophole in it. This is the kind of detective story that never gets told by mystery writers, probably because the leg work is almost as tedious as reading about it. But I am proud to say that the public prosecutor asked more and more that I be assigned to cases in which he was especially interested.

Take the case of Teodoro Domrique, a tough young Filipino ex-pugilist who went into the Asahi Cafe in the Honolulu suburb of Kaimuki on the night of February 17, 1936, and quietly ordered fish. Domrique, or Joe Doro, as he had been known to ring fans, was as crazy as a bedbug. He had been judged so by competent medical authorities.

But that night in the Asahi Cafe there was nothing to mark Joe Doro as an insane man. He went unnoticed by two other diners—Nelson Barrus, who worked at the Mutual Telephone Company exchange nearby, and Patrolman Henry Kualii, a uniformed policeman taking his dinner break. Only the Japanese proprietor paid attention when Joe Doro went back to the kitchen to give directions about the way he wanted his fish cooked. All three diners ate their meals at separate booths.

Then, at about seven o'clock, a fourth man entered. He was another policeman but on sick leave, which explained the pink pajama top under his coat and the Japanese-style slippers worn informally by many islanders. This man was something a little special; he was Sergeant Henry Chillingworth, age forty-two, possibly the best-known officer in Honolulu. A famous athlete for many years, he had built a reputation on the force for efficiency, intelligence, and personal courage. Besides being an athlete and police officer, Chillingworth came from a prominent island family. His brother before him had been a famous police officer and later assistant prosecutor. Other members of the family were equally conspicuous public figures in the islands.

Chillingworth gave Barrus a friendly wave and slid into a seat alongside Patrolman Kualii, who asked politely, "How do you feel, sergeant?"

"A little better, thanks," answered Chillingworth. "I'm kind of weak though, but I'll be all right in a few days."

"Better take it easy," said the patrolman.

Chillingworth had stopped listening. He was looking at the Filipino who had just emerged from his booth across the room to pay his bill. What the policeman saw was a stocky brown man, five feet four inches tall, wearing a brown leather jacket, white trousers, and a dark felt hat.

Chillingworth whispered to the patrolman, "Isn't that the guy who escaped from Kaneohe* last month—what's his name—Domrique—Joe Doro?"

"That's it," said the patrolman. "I looked at him when I came in and thought I'd seen that face somewhere."

The sergeant was all business now.

"Go call headquarters to send the wagon," he told Kualii. "I'm going to arrest him."

He slid out of his seat and walked to the front of the restaurant

*Kaneohe, on Windward Oahu, was the location of the Territorial Hospital for the insane. It is now called the Hawaii State Hospital.

where Joe Doro had just paid fifteen cents for his meal to the waitress, Kazue [*sic*] Kazaki. Chillingworth, a big man who stood six feet, towered over Joe Doro as he said, "You're under arrest, Domrique, for escaping from the Territorial Hospital."

The little man looked up calmly.

"I no Domrique," he said, then added, "I like drink ice water. We go kitchen, please."

Chillingworth must have thought he had the prisoner under complete control. He led Joe Doro to the kitchen, and the waiter gave him a glass of water. Joe Doro took a sip, lowered the glass to the table, and dashed out the kitchen door into the back of an alley that opened onto 12th Avenue. Chillingworth was after him like a shot, yelling, "Stop! Stop!" Three passersby heard the shouts and joined in the chase up 12th Avenue, which in those days was very dimly lit.

"Stop or I'll shoot!" bawled the sergeant though he had no gun. When his slippers caused him to stumble, he kicked them off and ran barefoot.

Joe Doro not only ran faster, he ducked off 12th Avenue into a thicket of rock-strewn bougainvillea. Chillingworth dived into the rocks and brush after him. The three-man volunteer posse turned in at the front of a house near the thicket. This house was the residence of Captain Harry T. Lake, a retired police officer. The chase took them to the rear of the house from where the three could hear sounds of a violent struggle. A moment later, Chillingworth staggered out from behind the house, blood streaming from his throat and chest, and fell on Lake's lawn close to the sidewalk.

John Fernandez, one of the three, stayed with Chillingworth while Stephen Atkins and Charles Arnold, the other two, pursued the assailant, but to no avail. Then Arnold called the police.

Fernandez tried to make the dying man speak, but the flow of blood was too great and too fast. His life ended in a gurgle on Captain Lake's lawn. It was surprising that Chillingworth had been able to stagger out as far as he did, for he was cut to pieces. He had a deep slash severing his jugular vein along with most of his throat and another deep cut that extended across the left side of his chest to his abdomen.

In the house, Captain Lake, who was an invalid, had been roused by the commotion. He heard someone say, "He's been stabbed." At that, the retired policeman telephoned Detective Lieutenant John Troche, then went out in the front yard with his wife, a trained nurse. They saw Chillingworth sprawled on the lawn beside the driveway. Mrs. Lake could see that he was dead. Police arrived in numbers almost immediately and surrounded the house.

The killer didn't remain free for long. With police on the alert all over town, a tip came to headquarters that Joe Doro was in the Bronx Hotel on Fort Street. Ten minutes later, at 9:40 P.M., five policemen arrested him in his room at the hotel. He offered no resistance. He was dressed in a white, blood-flecked shirt, clean dungarees, and unshined shoes. In the hip pocket of his dungarees police found a bloody clasp-knife with a four-and-a-half-inch blade.

Interrogation of the little ex-pugilist brought no results at all. While a ring of police stood around him, he stared down at his bloodstained shirt and slowly shook his head to all questions, though he admitted ownership of the knife to Captain McIntosh, who carried on the chief burden of the questioning.

"I no kill cop," Joe Doro insisted. "I see cops tonight first time in Bronx Hotel."

Everybody eventually got into the act, from Police Chief W. A. Gabrielson on down, including detectives and newspaper reporters. Joe Doro just stuck out his chin and calmly gave them all the same answer, "I no kill cop. I no kill anybody." That's the way it went, hour after hour. Finally, Joe Doro clammed up and quit answering questions.

The killing of a policeman arouses any community, and the killing of a policeman as prominent and popular as Henry Chillingworth multiplies the intensity by many degrees. Late that night, John C. Kelley, public prosecutor, took a crack at questioning the little brown man. He had no more luck than anyone else. Then he asked that I be assigned to the case. His request was granted, though most of the detectives in the division thought it was, as we say in Hawaii, "waste time."

"Take it easy," one of them told me. "What's the use? They'll just turn him back into the booby hatch anyhow. He's nuts. He's already been found insane. They can't try him for murder."

"This case has got the town all upset," I answered. "They'll go for an indictment. You watch."

I started with the report on the questioning of Joe Doro, which went back into his past history, and got the answers pretty straight on the salient points. First coming to Hawaii eight years before, he had gone to Kauai to work. Four years later, he had come back to Oahu. That was in 1931. He told McIntosh that he and three companions had broken into a second-hand store downtown and were later arrested, convicted, and sentenced to a twenty-year prison term.

Then he had been adjudged insane and was committed to Kaneohe hospital on August 22, 1935. On January 1, 1936, he had escaped. He told Captain McIntosh he had stayed around Kaneohe for the next three days, begging for food from friends. Then he had come to the Palama district of Honolulu, a slum area, and hid out for two weeks more. He had slept on a bench and continued to beg for food. Captain McIntosh tried to get the names of people who helped him, but Joe Doro claimed he couldn't remember any of them. He did say he had gone to Waialua and got a job feeding pigs for a Japanese man. After two weeks of that, he had come back to Honolulu with seven dollars in his pocket. From that point, the questioning was all downhill.

"Where did you get the knife?" he was asked.

"I found it in Kalihi."

"Where did you get the clothes you are wearing? These are not Kaneohe institution clothes."

"I broke into my locker at Hawaiian Pine (a cannery where he had worked before his arrest) two weeks ago and took them."

"Isn't it a fact that three days ago you went to work for a Korean man named Kong on Sierra Drive?"

"No," Joe Doro answered with emphasis.

"Isn't it a fact that Monday morning you left there with $93 belonging to your employer, Kong?"

"No."

"Then where did you get the $78 we found on you when you were arrested tonight?"

"I found him in Kalihi. I not tell lie."

"Where have you been all day?"

"Around Palama."

"What did you eat tonight in the Asahi Cafe?"

"I not in Kaimuki today. I eat in restaurant near Luzon Tailor Shop in Palama."

"You were seen in the Asahi Cafe tonight. Two police officers saw you there."

Joe Doro shook his head. "No. I no see officers there. Only at Bronx Hotel."

"How did the blood get on the knife?"

"I have nose bleed."

"When?"

"Last week."

"How does it happen, then, that this blood and the blood in your hat is still wet?"

Joe Doro quit talking and just looked down at his shirt. When told that he would be confronted with witnesses who saw him at the Asahi Cafe and in Kaimuki, he stuck out his chin and said, "Let them come see me. Then you see I no lie to you."

It was obvious we would get no help from Joe Doro. Then the investigation took on added importance. Three days after Sergeant Chillingworth died, Dr. Frederick E. Trotter, president of the Territorial Board of Health, appointed Dr. Richard E. Kepner, Dr. F. H. Tong, and Dr. R. K. Chun, together with Dr. A. B. Eckhard, psychiatrist at the hospital, to re-examine Joe Doro's mental condition. Two days later, they reported: "We are now of the opinion that at the present time he, Domrique, alias Joe Doro, is having a lucid interval, in which state he can determine right from wrong, and that there was that time [of the murder] no mental disease which could affect any criminal possibility."

Joe Doro was sent to a cell at Oahu Prison and the investigation became almost a twenty-four-hour-a-day proposition. I worked with two other detectives, Richard Stevens and Felipe Corpus.

The indictment by the Territorial grand jury on March 7 was easy enough. But when Judge H. E. Stafford appointed O. P. Soares as attorney to defend Joe Doro, we knew that we had our work cut out for us. No defense attorney in the islands had a higher reputation for snatching men from the gallows or opening prison doors for his clients.

We tried once more to grill Joe Doro himself, but he stuck to the same answer, "I no kill cop." Now our only alternative was to reconstruct the whole day of the killing, beginning early that morning. It was slow, methodical work, like placing one brick upon another to build a house. But, unlike a bricklayer, we could not run down to the supply company and buy evidence. We had to go out and dig for it. Even though we knew where to look, hours and hours of leg work were involved. It's a job that requires painstaking thoroughness and attention to detail. We went out and found witnesses who could account for every minute of Joe Doro's actions on the day of the killing.

At 6:30 A.M. on the day of the crime, he was fired from a temporary job as gardener by Chee Soon Kong, partly because Kong suspected him of stealing $93 from his home.

At 10 A.M. Doro left Kong's residence. He carried a bundle of clothes.

At 11 A.M. he asked a taxi driver in Kaimuki where he could find a room nearby.

A little after 11 A.M. Doro left a bundle of clothes at a tailor shop in Kaimuki and asked for a room. He was told there was none available.

At 11:30 A.M. he stopped at the shop of a Kaimuki shoemaker to have new rubber heels put on his shoes. The shoemaker identified the shoes as those Doro was wearing when arrested.

Before noon Doro stopped at the barber shop of Saburo Furoyama to get a "shieky" haircut.

At 2 P.M. he bought a fifteen-cent ticket at the Kaimuki Theater and entered for the matinee. John B. Mills, the theater manager, saw Doro leave the theater and cut across the grounds of Liliuokalani School.

Shortly before 7 P.M. he entered the Asahi Cafe, walked back to

106

the kitchen and told the cook, Keichi Uchihara, how he wanted his fish cooked.

Then came the chase and death of Sergeant Chillingworth near 12th Avenue.

Shortly after 7 P.M. Joe Doro was back at the tailor shop, disheveled, excited, to pick up his bundle of clothes and hurry off.

A few minutes after that he jumped on the running board of a taxi at a stand in Kaimuki and shouted, "Drive me to Palama quick!" The taxi had a load. Doro found another, which took him and his bundle of clothes across Honolulu to the junction of Liliha and Vineyard streets.

About 8 P.M. a woman saw a Filipino enter a garage on Vineyard Street opposite Waipa Lane and remain there for half an hour. She called police. Captain Dewey O. Mookini arrived a few minutes later. He saw the man and gave chase, but lost him in a maze of alleyways.

I was on call that night. When the woman's telephone message came in to the station, I jumped into the car of Detective Jack Bothelo and rode to the garage with him. We got there just after the futile chase. Mookini was making a search. He found a bundle of bloody clothes with a hat on top that had blood inside. It appeared that Joe Doro had met a friend at the garage who brought him clean clothes and that he had changed there. We took the clothes to headquarters along with a fifteen-cent stub of a Kaimuki Theater ticket we found in one of the pockets.

At about 8:30 P.M. Joe Doro hired a taxi in the Liliha area and had himself driven to the Fujii Hat Shop where he claimed to have left a hat to be cleaned. The proprietor would not give him the hat when he could not produce a check. Next, the taxi drove him to a store where he bought a pie. The taxi driver said Joe Doro ate the pie "with great relish" while being driven to the Bronx Hotel.

With Doro's actions accounted for, we went to work on the bundle of clothes, identifying each article one way or another—by cleaners, tailors, relatives, or acquaintances—as belonging to Doro. The initials "B. A." on a shirt in the bundle seemed mysterious at first. But we found a cousin of Joe Doro, Benigno Aquias, from the island of Molokai, to testify he had loaned the shirt to Doro. Aquias also identified the bloody hat found at the garage on Liliha Street as one Joe Doro had swiped from a rack in a downtown restaurant.

A tailor-made shirt from the bundle had unusual stitching. I looked through old pictures taken of Joe Doro at headquarters on occasions when he had been arrested on drunk charges and suspicion of burglary. In one of the photos he was wearing the shirt. Prosecutor Kelley made a life-size enlargement of that picture to show the jury along with the shirt.

By the time we came to trial, we had 105 witnesses to put on the stand, plus much additional evidence. But Kelley closed his case after presenting only 50 witnesses. I guess he thought their testimonies were getting repetitious. Joe Doro sat through the trial looking as though he didn't care. He had sublime confidence in his attorney. Every day John Kelley made the offer to Soares that he would accept a plea of guilty of second-degree murder. Every day Soares would relay the offer to Joe Doro and urge him to accept the offer and save his neck.

"No," Joe Doro would answer. "I not guilty. I no kill cop. If they hang me, it will be your fault."

Soares didn't call any witnesses. Instead, he moved for a directed verdict of not guilty on the grounds that the prosecution had failed to show premeditation, also that the prosecution had failed to give evidence that Joe Doro was sane at the time of the killing. Both motions were denied.

But the trial wasn't over, not with a spellbinder like Soares in charge of the defense. In his argument, the attorney blamed authorities at the Kaneohe hospital and the police for Sergeant Chillingworth's death. The hospital authorities had allowed an insane man to escape and the police had failed to catch him. Soares was in top form as he derided the police, whose principal activities, he said, consisted of "wearing Sam Browne belts, having their fingernails manicured, and permitting prostitution to flourish in the community."

The tactic may have had some effect, because the jury came back with a verdict of guilty but only in the second degree. Mr. Soares was complimented on having pulled another man from certain death on the gallows. I got some nice praise from Prosecutor Kelley and from Jan Jabulka of the *Star-Bulletin*, who nicknamed me Dan Dunn after a sleuth of the comic strips. Jabulka said the nickname was "sincere tribute to dogged gumshoe work in the current criminal case."

But Joe Doro slid out of the clutches of the law in spite of all my work to put him away. In December of the same year he died in Queen's Hospital of what they called inflammation of the brain. His lucid interval was over.

13

Polynesians Play Rough

As the years passed, Chief Gabrielson and I came to like each other less and less for reasons, I believe, that had nothing to do with my being busted for drinking. I'll admit I didn't have much respect for the chief. When John Kelley, the prosecutor, asked more often for me to be assigned to his office to investigate cases, I saw a way out.

That's the way it happened. Eventually, Kelley asked to have me assigned to his office. Gabrielson acceded to the request. On April 16, 1936, he called me in before I moved from police headquarters up to the prosecutor's office in City Hall.

"You won't be needing your sergeant's badge up there," he said.

I laid my badge on his desk and he slid a detective's badge back over the desk to me. Right there I lost $10 a month in pay, but I didn't kick even though I was raising a family. I figured it was worth it to get out from under Gabrielson.

At the prosecutor's office, I joined another veteran detective, Val Cederlof, who had also run afoul of Gabrielson. The police chief had fired Val for reasons not much stronger than my permanent demotion.* Val had been snapped up by the prosecutor as a special investigator. He was beyond Gabrielson's reach while I was still on the force.

*Val Cederlof's obituary in the August 31, 1958, *Star-Bulletin* states that he joined the Police Department on May 15, 1921, as an examiner of chauffeurs and a detective. He was assigned to the prosecutor's office on February 1, 1933, then joined that office permanently on May 1, 1935, after resigning from the Police Department. This editor could not find a record of why he left the department. Like Jardine, Cederlof seems to have been an individualist. In 1926, during prohibition, he was fined $50 for taking a punch at a customs guard after coming off the passenger liner *S.S. President Wilson* under the influence of liquor and with a bottle in his pocket.

The work we did for the prosecutor was somewhat different from that of a police detective in that Val and I were usually not called into a case until a suspect had been charged.* Our job was to fill out the investigation and make sure the prosecutor had a solid case. The work gave us a little bit of stature, quite a bit of freedom, and considerable satisfaction when we were able to get a conviction.

The murder of Raymond Kaluahine on May 4, 1936, is a fairly good example because it received a lot of notoriety at the time, Kaluahine being one of the best-known football players in the islands. The year before, Glenn S. "Pop" Warner, famous Stanford coach, had brought a team of All-Stars down to play against the local talent, and the giant Hawaiian tackle had torn his line to shreds. Warner called him the best football player he had seen on the trip.

Amateur and high school football, played in the old wooden Honolulu Stadium at King and Isenberg streets, provided a lot of excitement in those days. Kaluahine had started playing football when a student at Kamehameha Schools, then played for the McKinley Alumni in the Senior League, the closest Hawaii had to professional football. When he jumped from the McKinley Alumni to the Town Team in 1935, the controversy that followed the move almost broke up the league. For a living, he drove a tractor for the Mutual Telephone Company, a firm that always employed many Hawaiians.

On the night of May 4, he was trying to sleep in his home on Ladd Lane in the shadow of Punchbowl Crater, but the noise from a drinking party down the street at a neighbor's house kept him awake. Kaluahine got out of bed and headed for the party, though

*Dan Liu, who served as chief of police from 1948 to 1969 and who had worked with John Jardine in the Police Department before then, said it was the practice of the public prosecutor at that time to hire special investigators because they could spend more time on cases than detectives in the Police Department. He said he remembers no rivalry between the special investigators and the departmental detectives. Instead, the special investigators were considered highly professional, and Jardine commanded "lots of respect" in the Police Department. Liu said, "Jardine was one who wouldn't let go. He was like a bulldog. And he was very good at details. I learned a lot from him." Personal communication, February 14, 1983.

not for festive purposes. There was a lot of uninhibited singing and shouting and hula dancing at the house of John Kahalewai, a couple of doors away. Thirty to forty people were present including a number of Samoans.

What happened next is hard to sort out. It seems that when Kaluahine asked the revelers to quiet down they offered him a drink, which he accepted. Then, somehow, a fight started with Kaluahine in the middle of it. The fight turned into a free-for-all, Samoans on one side, Hawaiians on the other. The Samoans apparently got the better of the battle. There were indications that sticks, clubs, and bottles were used in addition to fists and feet. Finally the neighbors put in a riot call for the police.

Officers found Samoans in bloody shirts leaving the scene and Hawaiians, some with bloody heads, who had been beaten by the Samoans. There was still fighting in little groups, and before order could be restored, a number of men had to be handcuffed to telephone poles. Then the police found the much-battered and all-but-lifeless body of Raymond Kaluahine in the yard, surrounded by debris of the fight. The athlete was rushed to the emergency hospital, but he died ten minutes after arrival without regaining consciousness. He had suffered a fractured nose, a broken jaw, a number of teeth knocked out, and contusions on the head.

Police were told that four Samoans had taken off in a taxi. They chased the taxi down and arrested all four. But they got little satisfaction from questioning them or the other guests. Now that the riot had been quieted and there was a corpse to explain, no one seemed to know anything for certain. One witness said Kaluahine had gotten into an argument with one of the Samoans while standing on the lanai. The Samoan, also a giant of a man, had struck the big football player, said this witness, knocking him from the lanai to the ground. Then he stood over the fallen man and yelled for someone to bring water to revive him. About this time the free-for-all started inside the house, said the witness, and the Samoan was left alone with Kaluahine.

The cops knew they hadn't got explanations for all the injuries Kaluahine had received, so they kept on digging. Detectives Leon Strauss, Jr., and Hugh Whitford, inspecting the area, found three of his teeth and a piece of lumber, maybe pulled off a sawhorse, that looked as though it might have been used as a club.

A neighbor from down the street, attracted by the noise, said he had watched from the road while a man stood over Kaluahine as the athlete lay on the ground and kicked him twice in the head. Another witness saw one of the Samoans yank a heavy board from a sawhorse nearby and begin attacking Hawaiians. Police released two of the suspects from the taxi but intensified questioning of the other two, Robert Auelua and Toa Hall, with the result that each vigorously accused the other of striking the fatal blow. But who could tell which was telling the truth? They were both charged with manslaughter.

At this point, it became another job tossed into the laps of Val Cederlof and me. Together with Edward N. Sylva, the deputy prosecutor, we started trying to make some sense out of the jumble before presenting the case for grand jury action.

We began by going back to the neighborhood for a house-to-house canvass, looking for new evidence. Our legwork paid off. We found three new witnesses, including a former detective and his son. The former detective told us that, from what he had seen, the four men in the taxi had beaten up Kaluahine before leaving.

Val and I went to work on our two suspects. One of them gave us a new picture of the case. We learned that all four men from the taxi had been held together in the bullpen at headquarters after being picked up. They were loosely guarded. Talking in Samoan they laid a plan, agreeing that two of the four would take the blame and relieve the other two so they could be released. But neither was taking the blame individually. We went out and picked up the other two men who had been in the taxi on the night of the murder. Yet, we were still no closer to finding out what had really happened. None of the Samoans was about to confess that he did it.

We went to work on them individually to break through their plan of defense, using a tactic as old as warfare. We tried to get one of them to double-cross the others and save his own skin. Finally, with Sylva making the offer of a reduced charge in return for turning state's evidence, Robert Auelua agreed to go before the grand jury and indict the others. As a result of his testimony, all four men were charged on June 12 with second-degree murder.

That pretty well broke the case open. On July 3, with Sylva's consent, Auelua pleaded guilty to manslaughter. The trial began on July 27 with selection of the jury for the case of the other three. On the following day, even before selection of the jury was finished, the three remaining suspects suddenly pleaded guilty to manslaughter, again with the consent of the prosecutor. Judge H. E. Stafford sentenced all four to ten years in Oahu Prison. They were committed immediately.

Sylva then made a statement describing the crime as nearly as we had recreated it from our evidence and the testimony of Auelua. It may not have been exact in all details, but it made more sense than any other single version. The *Star-Bulletin* quoted the statement that afternoon. The story read:

"Between thirty and forty men were participating in a beer party at 2003-B Ladd Lane. As the hour grew late the party grew noisy and Kaluahine appeared asking the merrymakers to quiet down. He stayed and had a few beers.

"Kaluahine made a remark to the effect that he didn't like the look of Toa Hall. To which Auelua replied, 'He's the champion boxer of Samoa.' Kaluahine retorted, 'Nobody can put my shoulders to the ground but maybe he can give me some lessons.'

"With that, Kaluahine, Auelua and Hall left the house and went outside, Hall and Kaluahine taking sparring positions. Then Auelua stepped in and struck Kaluahine, knocking him to the ground. From there, things happened quickly. William Wallwork and Telemu Leasau joined in the affray, some of the assailants striking Kaluahine with sticks while others kicked him.

"There followed a free-for-all which caused such a racket that neighbors called for the police. Kaluahine was taken to the emergency hospital where he died.

"Investigations by police resulted in the arrest of Auelua and Hall. Inquiries made later by Val Cederlof and John Jardine, detectives in the public prosecutor's office, connected the other two men with the crime."

14

The Headwaiter Who Never
Came Home

THE newspapers mentioned Val and me now and then when it was our work that led to a conviction. As time went on, I think we built a pretty good reputation around town as investigators. This may have annoyed Gabrielson somewhat. He tried several times to get me back to headquarters, but Kelley and every other prosecutor who succeeded him refused the request, in a nice way, of course, saying I was essential where I was. Without that kind of support, I would have been back under Gabrielson's thumb, because I was technically still a policeman and subject to orders from the chief at any time.

There was one case in which the chief's annoyance surfaced in public. It began at 4 A.M. on March 1, 1938, when one Mrs. Yaeko Takara awoke as usual in her modest apartment and was startled to find that her husband was not in bed. A glance around the room told her he had not come home the night before.

Matsusuke Takara, thirty-eight, her husband, was headwaiter at the Beach Walk Inn, a good second-class restaurant in Waikiki. He often stayed out late to drink with friends after work or to take in some sports event. Mrs. Takara was accustomed to his coming home and going to bed without waking her. She was not accustomed to not finding him in bed in the morning when she woke up.

She cooked breakfast for her brother, a carpenter at Hickam Field, then went next door to ask a neighbor to take her to Waikiki to look for her husband. They drove to the Beach Walk Inn and a couple of other places where Takara liked to drink. The places were closed. There was no sign of him. They returned home and the neighbor drove to work.

Mrs. Takara telephoned another man, a close friend of her husband, in another part of town. He came quickly in his car. They drove to the police station and to the emergency hospital. Finding no record of Takara, they returned home again. The distraught woman suggested they make a check on foot of the route Takara usually took on his way home. So they picked up another mutual friend, went back to Waikiki, and started looking.

In those days, the area on McCully Street between Kalakaua Avenue and the Ala Wai Canal was nothing but lantana and kiawe bushes. The anxious trio proceeded along McCully Street in the early morning, ignoring the traffic of people going to work, poking in the bushes, and looking for some sign of the vanished headwaiter.

Finally, Mrs. Takara saw a spot of familiar brown color in the bushes. Suddenly afraid, she turned and called to the nearest friend on the other side of the street. Together they approached. Now they could see that the spot of brown was Matsusuke's jacket and that he lay still among the kiawe. The wife saw that her husband lay on his back, his features smeared with blood and mud.

"Taka!" she called out, touching the battered head.

There was no movement. The head was cold to the touch. Mrs. Takara broke into tears as she accepted the reality of her husband's death. One of her friends opened his handkerchief to spread it over the dead man's face. The widow, sobbing, barely able to control herself, stood watch over the body with one friend while the other went to call the police.

Detectives Perry Parker and Roland Barringer and Sergeant Coxhead arrived first. They found a crowd of curious people already grouped around the body and the weeping widow. The policemen moved the people back and proceeded to examine the body and its immediate surroundings.

The dead man was wearing white shoes, blue and white socks, no garters, brown trousers, brown leather belt, brown flannel jacket with a zipper down the front, and a light polo shirt. The corpse lay on its back, right arm extended with fist clenched, left arm parallel to the body and the hand open. One leg was bent beneath the other leg. Blood had coagulated on the right eyebrow, nose, and ear. Mud was smeared heavily on the face, hands, and clothing. The body was stiff and cold.

Six and a half feet away, the detectives found a twenty-dollar bill, a couple of gum wrappers, and a streetcar token. A little farther away were a wallet, a pocket comb, and a book of matches. Underneath the body was a one-dollar bill, a silver dollar, and some change in silver amounting to $4.77. The total in currency and coins amounted to $26.77.

The detectives also noted that the ground immediately around the body had been trampled enough to indicate the possibility of a violent struggle. But because so many people had already viewed the body at close range, the police were unable to form any conclusions from that fact. Photographs were taken of the body and scene, and diagrams made. Then the body was picked up by the morgue wagon and hauled to the City morgue. The grief-stricken widow was escorted back to her home where she told the story you have read.

At the morgue, the body was examined more thoroughly. Dr. David Liu, assistant city and county physician, washed away the mud to discover that Takara's frontal jaw had been broken and his teeth knocked in. The face and lips were swollen, the left eye, left cheek, and lips were cut, and there was a shallow laceration on the right side of the forehead, as well as bruises on the neck and upper left shoulder.

Dr. Thomas Mossman, the city physician who did the postmortem, found a peculiar impression on the neck which could have been made, the doctor said, by the expansion octagon link band of a wristwatch on the arm of the killer. Opening the body, Mossman found the sternum bruised, three ribs broken on both left and right sides, the chest filled with blood, and the lungs collapsed. The ribs were probably broken, the doctor said, while Takara was lying on his back and his killer or killers had either jumped on him or stomped him. Inside the head, the doctor found no fractures, but the brain showed hemorrhages on top, there was an injury behind one temple and a severe concussion at the back of the skull. The doctor said he believed strangulation had contributed to the death of the waiter, for he found broken cords on the left side of the throat.

That was the beginning of the Takara murder case. It was far from being the biggest sensation in the annals of Honolulu crime, the victim being of humble origin and circumstance. Yet, when the news broke in the newspapers, it set the town on its ear. The case coupled brutality and mystery in a way that made people talk about it. Takara's own character had something to do with it. Like many another headwaiter, he was known to many people and liked by virtually all of them. He was especially liked by his fellow workers and acquaintances. One young waiter almost wept as he told police how Takara, without children of his own, had treated him like a son and had taken him to boxing matches.

The pathos of the bereaved widow added to the tragedy. On March 2, reporters found her at home praying before a Buddhist altar lighted with candles, her husband's ashes in a black-draped urn at one side. She put down her Buddhist beads to answer questions and tell the newsmen she knew of no enemies her husband might have had.

"I pray they will find whoever did this thing," she said. "He must be made to pay for his crime."

Word came down in the Police Department that Chief Gabrielson was anxious to solve the murder. One reason was because this crime had attracted the close attention of a Japanese–English language newspaper, the *Hawaii Hochi*. The *Hochi,* always accusing the police of laxity and inefficiency, had great influence in the Japanese community. The lively portraits created by its cartoonists and editorial writers, not all Japanese, had appreciative readers in all Honolulu, even in offices of the big companies on Merchant and Fort streets.

Chief Gabrielson wanted action. He had every available man follow such clues as there were and hunt for new ones. Takara's fellow waiters were interviewed, with meager results. The detectives traced Takara's movements as best they could. February 28, the day before his death, had been payday. He had received $34.42 in an envelope from his boss, then proceeded to a nearby cafe to have a bottle of Kirin beer and two Scotch-and-sodas. From there he went to a chop suey restaurant on John Ena Road to have a couple more and left about 11 P.M. At 12:10, shortly after closing time, he had come back to the chop suey place for another drink, but the waitress turned him away saying it would be illegal to serve him. He nodded understandingly and headed up John Ena Road toward Kalakaua—and to his death.

In spite of Gabrielson's impatience, nothing more happened until twenty days after the murder. A waitress in a sandwich shop on John Ena Road told police that some time after midnight on March 1, the night of the murder, she had waited on two men in a car and that one of them, dressed in an aloha shirt, was messy, his face covered with blood and dirt. He had a bruise on the right side of his forehead that was cut open a little. The waitress said she didn't know either of the men by name but she was acquainted informally with the one in the aloha shirt because she had danced with him quite often at the Rendezvous Dance Hall, an establishment also on John Ena Road. She had commented on his condition and asked him what happened. He said he had been in a fight.

After hearing her story, police arrested the two men, soldiers stationed at Fort Ruger, Private Sol Minolek and Private Walter Mearns (as I shall call them here) and took them to headquarters. Minolek, the one in the aloha shirt, said he and Mearns had gone to the dance at the Rendezvous on the night in question to wait for another soldier. Minolek's license plates, being those of the year before, would expire that night, the last day of February 1938. If he were caught by police driving after midnight on March 1, he stood a good chance of being stopped and given a traffic ticket. But if the car were not moving under its own power he would be safe.

So, shortly after midnight, a Private Beryl Boise and a girl came in Private Willie Jeeter's car to tow Minolek and Mearns back to the post. But at Paki and Monsarrat avenues, Minolek told police, the tow rope broke. He decided to take a chance and drive the rest of the way by his own motor. Boise and the girl pulled on ahead, Minolek said, but not before he took a wristwatch from the girl and put it on his own wrist. He asked Boise to drive her home and then bring the car back to the post because he wanted to use it.

When he got the car Boise had been driving, he and Mearns drove to the sandwich shop. Minolek said he had been driving in the warm night without a shirt. Now, before he went into the sandwich shop, he got out of the car and put his aloha shirt back on. Pulling the shirt over his head, he said, he lost balance and fell blindly, striking his head on the ground and receiving the injury over his right eye. After visiting the sandwich shop, Minolek said, he drove around for awhile, then over to his girl friend's house on 6th Avenue, and finally back to the post.

Police asked Minolek and the others about a fight, but could get no confirmation of any such incident from them. Sergeant Alfred Fraga was brought to take pictures of the marks on Minolek. The photos showed a scratch scar on the nipple of the right side of Minolek's chest, another scratch partly healed on the right hand between the thumb and index fingers, a large bruise scar on the right eye, a small prick mark at the back of the right arm, and bruised knuckles on the right hand.

Still Minolek insisted that he had got some of the injuries when he fell on the ground; the others he didn't remember. Detectives took him out to demonstrate how he had fallen down. When he tried to do it over again, he did it so poorly that the detectives were convinced it couldn't have happened. Mearns said he had been sitting in the car at the time when Minolek fell, but in such a position that he couldn't see the actual fall. He did say he had seen Minolek pick himself up from the ground, though.

After more intensive questioning, Minolek told detectives he had worn Jane Kealoha's wristwatch without taking it off until 6 A.M., March 1. He led detectives to his footlocker at the fort, took the watch out and turned it over to them. It was a lady's wristwatch of yellow metal, octagon in shape. The band was also of yellow metal with an octagon shape and was broken at the clasp. There were cracks in the crystal. Minolek was very evasive when police questioned him about damage to the watch.

Detective Alexander Rice stretched the links of the watch to compare them with the impressions on Takara's throat as shown in the photographs. The links matched the marks on Takara's throat. Later that same afternoon, detectives took the watch to Dr. Mossman for a microscopic examination for any skin or blood that might have adhered to the watch and chain. The doctor reported a couple of days later that the tests had brought negative results.

Another witness came in with a story police thought might be a lead. A Japanese man had been sitting at a *saimin* (Japanese noodle) stand on John Ena Road late on the night of the murder when he saw Takara pass on the street outside in company with a white man. The witness remembered the approximate time, which was after the bar had turned Takara away. That meant this witness was the last person to see the headwaiter alive. Who was the *haole* walking along John Ena Road? The Japanese described him only as of medium size and dressed in a dark suit.

There were no more new developments after that. The soldiers didn't change their answers no matter how much they were questioned. The police let them go.

About this time, newspaper reporters began asking questions that indicated they hadn't much faith in the steps being taken to find the murderer. They asked Prosecutor Charles E. Cassidy if Val Cederlof and I would be assigned to the case. Mr. Cassidy told them he "would be glad to do anything to help" and we could be assigned to the case if it were desirable.

That statement must have got under Chief Gabrielson's skin. He told reporters the next day, "Our men are just as qualified as his (Cassidy's). Detectives Jardine and Henry Silva (also assigned to the prosecutor's office) are members of the Police Department. It is their duty to turn over to us any tips which they may come across." Gabrielson explained the failure of the police to solve the crime as the result of a lack of "material evidence." Usually, he said, there is a gun or a knife or some weapon or other evidence to go on. In this instance, he said, there was nothing like that. "The only way we can solve this case is by a tip-off or a break," he said.

That's how it remained until Val Cederlof and I were assigned to the case seventeen years later. What happened then will be told in its place. In the meantime, a lot of water flowed under the bridge. Some of it was a little dirty.

15

"He Was a Real Nice Boy,"
the Neighbors Said

PUNAHOU SCHOOL in the 1940s was where the wealthy and aristocratic families sent their sons and daughters to prepare them for college, usually on the mainland. So when old Mrs. Mamie Piper, mother of Punahou's superintendent of buildings and equipment, paused in a shortcut across the lawn while shepherding two of her grandchildren home at 10:40 on the night of October 2, 1949, she was shocked to see what looked to her like a drunk sprawled out under an oleander bush. As soon as she got home, she indignantly told her son, Francis Piper. He got in his truck and hastened to eject the interloper.

Piper drove to the oleander bush his mother had described. Sure enough, the headlights of his truck picked up the supine figure of a man. Piper stopped his vehicle to proceed on foot. Drawing close, he saw the man was Caucasian, wearing a bright aloha shirt and khaki pants. He was sprawled on his back. Piper took him for a soldier from Schofield Barracks, or maybe Hickam Field, who had somehow wandered up to Punahou from some bar and flopped under the oleander bush to sleep it off.

The superintendent, muttering to himself, kicked the figure lightly on the leg. The sleeper did not waken. He didn't even stir. Piper bent over for a closer look. He observed bruises, skinned places, and what looked like spots of blood mixed in with the night-blooming cereus design on the yellow aloha shirt. The man wasn't drunk. He was dead. And from the signs he saw, Superintendent Piper had the chilling suspicion he'd been killed.

Piper hastily walked back to his truck and blinked the headlights in the direction where he knew Ray Leggett would be walking his watch. Leggett was an accountant with the school and also a special officer who assumed the role of a relief watchman on Sunday nights. When he saw what Piper pointed out to him, he drove to one of the school buildings and called the police.

That was the way they found the body of Private Elvin J. Vidrine, Company A, First Battalion, Schofield Barracks. Before they learned his name, the police probably knew a good deal more about him than his own family did. He was a slender man, age 20, weight 140 pounds. He had been savagely beaten about the head. But this was not the cause of death. Probably while Vidrine was unconscious, the murderer had garroted him with a narrow rope. A close examination by Dr. Alvin Majoska, Honolulu City and County coroner, revealed that Vidrine had probably been the passive recipient of an unnatural sex act described by legal and medical authorities as fellatio.

The Army was notified and officers and soldiers came in from Schofield to identify the body. Some pals told how they had hoisted a few drinks with Vidrine in a Hotel Street bar late in the afternoon before he was murdered. Finally the bartender had refused to serve him any more and he left. There the trail ended.

The cops spent some time taking prints of an automobile tire near the bush and a shoe print that wasn't Vidrine's. That's all they could get on the case until a couple of weeks later when somebody knocked a sailor unconscious, stripped him of his clothes, and left him lying on a beach at Kulamanu Place, right in the shadow of Diamond Head. The sailor was alive, barely, but he had a fractured jaw along with quite a collection of bruises. His story gave police a lead in a new direction.

That direction is described in James Jones' book *From Here to Eternity,* in which he tells how servicemen without money to pay a prostitute's fee sometimes went to certain parts of Waikiki and had an evening's thrill without cost, possibly even a profit, by picking up a "queer." We Honolulu cops knew that what Jones wrote about the old Army at Schofield was true and is still true of the new Army.

In this case, only the sequence was different. The sailor had come to town from Pearl Harbor and had found his man at the corner of King and Nuuanu streets in downtown Honolulu. He had been driven to the home of his new friend "somewhere near a park" and they'd had a couple of drinks of Seagram's 7-Crown whiskey. Then his friend's parents had come home, so the two left the house and went to a bar in Waikiki. From there they took off for the beach at the end of Kulamanu Place off Diamond Head Road. There had been some homosexual love-making. The sailor didn't remember much after that. He had been knocked unconscious and he didn't quite know how. All he knew was that he had a mighty sore jaw and was happy to be alive, even though in an embarrassing condition.

The police began to fit other incidents into this pattern. They recalled a soldier who had been found nude close to the same place on September 11. He had taken his clothes off in preparation for the same sort of love-making. Suddenly the "queer" began to beat him with a stick and later, a stone. That was all the soldier remembered. Someone had pulled him out of the edge of the surf about 2 A.M. If he'd stayed there until the tide came in, he'd never have been able to tell the cops his story.

Five days later, on September 16, still another soldier had been picked up by police. He was conscious but minus his pants and with a fractured jaw and a big lump on his head. He said he had been picked up downtown, lured to an isolated area near a stream and hit on the side of the jaw and on the head with a stone. This man had been strong enough to retain consciousness and fight off his attacker. He and the sailor identified the attacker from mug shots of known homosexuals, picking out a young drugstore employee named Clarence Carvalho. Carvalho was taken into custody for questioning.

The quiet, slender young man admitted everything. He had been the assailant in all three cases, and he didn't mind going into detail to describe the love-making. He went into such detail that the police began to think he was some kind of nut. He seemed to take pleasure in confessing, though he couldn't give any reason for beating the servicemen up. It wasn't antipathy for the servicemen. He had served a couple of years in the Army himself. It all seemed to be tied up with his abnormal sex slant, which was complicated to say the least. Not only did he get a bang out of assaulting the servicemen after making love to them, but he also got a bang out of keeping articles of clothing he took from them. He still had a number of such articles at home.

The cops weren't concerned with his peculiar psychoses except to solve their own problems of the moment, the most pressing of which was the unsolved murder on the Punahou campus. And the solution seemed right around the corner. After Carvalho confessed, a couple of detectives had gone up to his home, taking along the soldier who had been pulled out of the surf and wanted to get back some of his clothes. The first thing the detectives knew, the soldier and Carvalho were shaking hands and all but sobbing on each other. Carvalho got so emotional he actually began weeping. Then he gave out with: "You might as well know. The soldier who was found on the Punahou campus—I put him there."

One of the detectives asked how he did it. The young man said he had strangled Vidrine with the cord from a venetian blind, performing the act at his home on Keeaumoku Street. They took Carvalho to the police station, the detective gave the story to his captain, and intensive questioning began. Carvalho said he had taken Vidrine to his home where they had drunk some Seagram's 7-Crown. Vidrine had got noisy. To quiet him, Carvalho said, he had gone out to his car, got the cord, had taken Vidrine by surprise and strangled him.

Then he had loaded him into the car, driven to the Punahou campus and put the body under the oleander bush, face down. Among other things Carvalho said in his statement, Vidrine had a GI web belt rolled up in his left hip pocket. He said he had taken Vidrine's wallet and thrown it over a stone wall on the opposite side of the street from where he put the body.

There is nothing the police like better than to solve a killing in a hurry. But the more this boy talked the more suspicious they got of his story. For one thing, he had Vidrine dressed in a green aloha shirt and blue trousers, whereas he had actually been wearing a yellow aloha shirt with a night-blooming cereus pattern, and khaki trousers. When they took him to Punahou to re-enact the crime, he picked the wrong gate as the one he had entered in his car. The gate he indicated had been chained up the night of the murder.

Then he pointed out where he had put the body, only he picked the wrong side of the bush. And he had the body lying face down, whereas it was found face up.

Besides, the boy seemed too anxious to confess. The detectives began to wonder if he was giving them details he'd read in the newspapers. They put a fingerprint man to work on his car and got the police chemist to test a cord found in the trunk to see if any connecting link could be established. The chemist came up with nothing on his early tries. So did the fingerprint man. That decided it for the chief of detectives. He told his men not to waste more time questioning Carvalho. He was just a nut, progressing quickly from the confessing to the boasting stage. He didn't even have his facts straight.

Cleared of murder, Carvalho had only to face the other charges of attacking servicemen. He came off lucky with those, because only one case was brought against him, two of the servicemen leaving the islands before their cases came up. Carvalho got off with a fifteen-dollar fine and a fifteen-day jail sentence which was suspended for thirteen months.

At the request of the captain of detectives, he was taken to the Territorial Hospital for observation. He entered the hospital on October 22, 1949, and was released June 30, 1950. On his release, the detectives questioned him a little once more about the Vidrine case. This time he denied knowing anything of it, and he seemed a lot more rational than when he'd confessed to the murder. It looked as though he had become reasonably well adjusted.

Dr. Marcus Guensberg, head of the hospital, submitted a report to the police that seemed to bear all this out. He said Carvalho was a confirmed homosexual who had been engaging in homosexual acts, active and passive, since the age of twelve. In all the sessions with psychiatrists at the hospital, Carvalho had done or said nothing to indicate he had any connection with the killing of Private Vidrine.

That's how the matter stood when our new police chief, Dan Liu, asked Val Cederlof and me to go over some of the old unsolved cases in the police files and see what we could come up with. The Vidrine case was about two and one-half years old when we inherited it. The first thing I did was study the record. I read and re-read the questions asked Carvalho and the answers he gave. Despite the discrepancies, there was one thing he said that he couldn't have read in the newspapers, something the detectives hadn't noticed. He had told them about the Army-type webbed belt Vidrine had rolled up in his left hip pocket. He couldn't have known about that unless he was the killer because it wasn't reported in the newspapers and only a few detectives had that information.

Once I spotted that item, I began reading the record again in a new light. What if Carvalho had deliberately mixed up the colors of the shirt and pants and where he put the body and which gate he entered, in order to confuse the detectives after he made the first slip? True, the chemist and the identification expert hadn't found anything to link Carvalho to the crime. But they hadn't found anything that ruled him out as the murderer, either. And they had been called off before they'd had a chance to finish.

The detectives hadn't made anything of the similarity between plaster casts made of two tire prints found near Vidrine's body and of the left front and right front tires of Carvalho's car. It was a proper decision because tires like Carvalho's could be found on hundreds of cars around Honolulu. But no effort had been made to match a shoeprint found on the scene against Carvalho's shoes. I felt that was an oversight. Also, no effort had been made to remove the new seat covers from Carvalho's car to test underneath for possible blood findings. Because by that time, the detectives had convinced themselves they had the wrong man.

With this in mind, I suggested we start the investigation all over again from the beginning. And we did. We went to the house on Keeaumoku Street where the Carvalhos had lived, only to find that another family had bought it and moved in. We found no clues outstanding. We traced the automobile through three new owners and found that it still carried the same seat covers Carvalho had put on. We made arrangements to remove and search underneath if necessary.

Then we went after Carvalho. We found him working at Pearl Harbor. With a Federal Criminal Investigation Department man along, we began questioning him casually. I did most of the talking. Before long, I discovered that I'd known his father back at a time when the elder Carvalho had been a taxi driver. It always helps to establish that kind of relationship when you can, and an old-timer in Honolulu can usually do it with the boys who come from here. We went into the assault cases to which he'd already confessed. He confessed all over again. But he had changed now, he assured us. He said he had confessed those crimes to his priest. That gave me the opening I was looking for.

"Did you confess to the priest about the Vidrine murder?" I asked him.

Immediately he froze up. He hadn't said anything to the priest, he answered, because he didn't know anything about the Vidrine murder.

That was the beginning of a long session of interrogation, often one of the least pleasant but most important part of a criminal investigation. We were in an office at the Pearl City police station and we stayed there all afternoon. I took Carvalho back over the statements he had made when he confessed before. Now he denied them. Once he got a little stormy and I had to talk a little rough in return.

"Look boy, don't get smart," I told him. "We've been acting like gentlemen to you and we expect you to act like one. Maybe someone else might put your head through that wall."

It had the desired effect, though of course I was bluffing. I certainly wasn't going to use any rough stuff. There isn't a thing in a criminal investigation you can get with muscle that you can't get better with brains and enough legwork. Carvalho quieted down. But he still wasn't confessing. He told us the chief of detectives had shaken his hand at the end of the police investigation and told him he was cleared. So what did we think we were going to find out?

By that time, we'd been at it for six hours. It was 7:30 in the evening. We decided to get dinner and try another session at our office in City Hall. We took Carvalho to a waterfront cafe and got to our office about 9 o'clock to start again. This time we had the documents at our fingertips—the reports of the detectives on the first time Carvalho confessed. But he still wasn't buying it. Finally I got down to the item I figured for my clincher.

"What about that web belt in Vidrine's left hip pocket?" I asked. "You knew about that. You're the only person who knew about that belt except the police who first searched Vidrine's dead body. You knew about it because you put the body there. You were the only one who could have known because the body was on its back. No one could have put that belt in the hip pocket after you left it there."

At first Carvalho denied he had ever made any such statement to the detectives. Then he said he didn't know what we were talking about. Finally he just sat and refused to say anything. His head dropped and he looked sullen. I went back to an item we'd been over before. What about the seat covers on his car? When had he put them on? He wasn't sure.

Then I jumped to his Army career. Did he serve in the Army? Yes. And he had been honorably discharged in 1948. Had he brought home any Army clothing? Yes, some sun tans. Did he still have them? No, he'd worn them out and thrown them away. Had he ever burned anything such as clothes around the Keeaumoku Street house? No. Had he taken any jewelry from Vidrine's body?

A moment of hesitation. Then, no, he didn't know anything about Vidrine's murder.

That's the way it went for two and a half more hours, until 11:30. We decided we'd have to give up for the night. The CID man knocked off, too. Investigator Souza drove us back toward the civilian housing area of Pearl Harbor where Carvalho lived. We would pick him up in the morning for further questioning.

It was a night I'll remember for a long time. Souza, a big, burly man, a veteran of World War II, drove. I sat in the front seat beside him. Carvalho sat in the rear seat with my companion in many a manhunt through the years, Val Cederlof. The highway ahead was a continuous stream of headlights. The black, warm Pacific night was all around us. Everything seemed relaxed and peaceful. We might have been four businessmen riding to our country homes after some late meeting or banquet, instead of a murder suspect and three detectives trying to get a confession out of him.

"You know, Clarence," I said without looking around, "deep down in your heart you know you murdered Vidrine. You'll have God to answer to." I paused for a moment and then asked in a normal tone without looking around, "You killed him, didn't you?"

"Yes," came the answer from the back seat.

I kept looking straight ahead and pretended I hadn't heard. I asked again, "You killed him, didn't you?"

"Yes," came the answer, louder this time.

With that, the dam was broken. All I had to do to get answers was to ask questions. Now the story came out straight. Carvalho had picked up Vidrine, or had been picked up, on Hotel Street in the downtown area of Honolulu. They had gone to Carvalho's home for some drinks. Since Carvalho's parents weren't home, they had the run of the house. They played some records, then sat out on the porch drinking Seagram's 7-Crown. Vidrine began to make advances and there was a little spat. Vidrine hit him, Carvalho said, and tore his shirt. Carvalho went out in the yard, picked up a coconut. He came back and hit Vidrine on the head with it. Carvalho called it self-defense. What he did next wasn't self-defense and Carvalho didn't want to talk about it until I asked him, "Did you hit him before or after you strangled him?"

"Before," was the answer. Then he told how he had dragged the body to his car and disposed of it under the oleander bush at about 8 P.M. This time he had the right gate.

I asked if he had confessed to anyone else. It turned out he had confessed the murder to his priest at the Fort Street Cathedral and also to his father during a visit his father had paid him at the hospital. The father had figured it out for himself after hearing of the assaults on the other servicemen. He'd asked young Carvalho if he'd killed Vidrine. The young man said he had, but didn't go into details, and his father told him not to tell anyone, not even his stepmother. I asked if his roommate at the housing area knew he had killed Vidrine.

"No," he said.

As we suspected, he had bought the new seat covers after the Vidrine killing. Carvalho would talk in spurts and then lapse into periods where he would say only yes or no. But he was cooperating right down the line, straightening up a lot of things that had made the cops discount his first confession.

The impact of it got to the young man a little bit at a time. He seemed more worried about the publicity he'd get among his friends and the repercussions on his parents than he did about any punishment he might get himself. He said his father had high blood pressure. Carvalho said he wanted to see his father and tell him he'd confessed, to break the news to him gently.

By that time it was 1:30 A.M. I did something I had done before in similar cases, something I've been criticized for more than once. I let Carvalho go home. All I had was his promise that he'd show up for an appointment with us next morning at 9:30. We would meet him at the fire hydrant in front of the building where he lived and go together to talk to his father. I didn't arrest him because he was trying to do a very human thing, to mitigate the awful effect of his crime. I have never been able to reject an appeal like that. Maybe I'm too soft-hearted to be a cop.

For awhile the next morning I thought I had taken one chance too many. Carvalho never showed up at the fire hydrant. We hunted every place we could think of and found him at last. He said he had been considering suicide. I learned later that he had also called an attorney.

The fight in court promised to be a stiff one. We prepared our case with pictures and documents. Then we got Governor Oren E. Long to help us influence Army authorities to bring back the witnesses we needed. They had been shifted all over the world since the murder, but the armed forces flew them back from Europe, Asia, and various parts of the United States. We were ready in mid-November when the trial began in the court of Judge Carrick E. Buck.

Carvalho's attorney, Arthur Trask, put up a vigorous defense at first, stating he would show that an Army captain, who had committed suicide a week after the Vidrine murder, had killed himself out of remorse over slaying Vidrine. But after the jury had been chosen and seven days of testimony taken, the defense attorney changed his mind and entered a plea of nolo contendere, no desire to contest. Judge Buck asked Carvalho if he understood the action his attorney was about to take. He answered that he did and entered his new plea. The judge then dismissed the jury.

On December 5, 1952, Judge Buck sentenced Carvalho to seventy-five years in prison for the crime of murder in the second degree. Thus ended a case the prosecutor called "one of the most vicious and sordid murders we have had in the Territory," perpetrated by a person his neighbors thought was a "real nice boy."

16

King of the Fleecers

THERE have been few confidence men whose legends equal
that of Alexander Teruji Sumida, a chunky native of Hiroshima,
Japan, who could barely speak English and who had some difficulty writing his own name. Sumida was given the title King of the
Fleecers by newspapermen, and he gloried in it.

From the standpoint of total amount taken from his victims he
wasn't the largest operator in Hawaii. But I think he deserves the
title because he earned it in the public mind and because he came
from such an unlikely background for a fleecer. Sumida struggled
for success in his brand of crime with as much energy as some men
struggle for success in legitimate business. At one time or another,
he succeeded in conning nearly everyone associated with him,
including the police and himself.

Perhaps his most amazing talent lay in his theatrical knack for
presenting himself in the character he desired to portray. A criminal on the mainland may move from state to state concealing his
identity and altering it to suit the occasion. In Honolulu and
throughout the islands, it is very difficult for anybody to appear
long in the eyes of associates as someone much different from what
he actually is. Yet Sumida, who had spent the earlier part of his life
in the islands as a laborer, seaman, carpenter, and bootlegger,
managed for years to convince his victims and even his friends that
he was a wealthy, retired businessman with an eye out for a good
deal.

The King of the Fleecers also possessed physical courage. Once a
gang of strong-arm men put him in a car and drove him around
Oahu threatening to kill him unless he told where he had hidden

some money. With a pistol to his head, Sumida remained calm and told his captors:

"I am an old man without much longer to live. It makes little difference to me if you shoot. But this is an island. If you think you can get away with it, you are foolish. The police will surely get you."

The strong-arm men gave up, finally, and drove the old fleecer back to Honolulu without harming a hair on his head.

Another time the police bunco squad had him in the interrogation room and were trying to crack him. With cops all around him shooting questions at him about his latest swindle, the chunky Japanese bore himself with dignity, as if he were in charge instead of the police. Then he raised a hand.

"You see these walls?" he asked. "When I die, these walls will never say that I, Alexander Teruji Sumida, talked. Where is your telephone? I want to call my lawyer."

It was all very impressive and the cops believed him.

This is not to excuse the harm he did. Fleecers and confidence men have often been pictured to the public as somehow less vicious than the criminal who robs at gunpoint. It is a view to which I cannot subscribe. I have never found a fleecer who had any mercy in his system. Far from being satisfied with taking part of what the victim has, he invariably urges the sucker to borrow on his house or car if necessary. Too often the fleecer's victim is an elderly person who can ill afford to part with his or her life's savings.

One of Sumida's marks was a Japanese man, a college graduate and manager of his mother-in-law's store. His marriage nearly broke up after he lost $16,000 in a bogus opium deal with Sumida. His mother-in-law threatened to fire him, his wife to divorce him, and on top of all that, he nearly suffered a nervous breakdown.

An older Japanese couple gave Sumida $13,000 in chunks of $7,000 and $6,000 to set up a phony *okolehao* still. When they discovered there was no still, both husband and wife suffered severe shock. The husband threatened to commit suicide. The wife said she followed him around for months to make sure he didn't carry out his threat. At the same time, the whole burden of running the store fell on her. She begged me later not to question her husband for fear that any mention of the swindle might bring on a mental relapse.

Neither I nor any other cop can take any real credit for Sumida's confession, though I got a letter of commendation from Chief of Police Dan Liu for directing the interrogation. So I will simply relate the confession in the order of events in Sumida's life as he told them to me over a period of days in a narrative that took on the aspects of *The Thousand and One Nights of Scheherazade*.

The future fleecer was born in Hiroshima on March 19, 1893, and was brought to the Hawaiian island of Kauai in 1907 by his father and step-mother. They came as immigrant laborers. As a boy of thirteen, Alexander wanted to go to school, but both his father and step-mother objected. Life was too hard for a struggling plantation family in those days to afford such a luxury. Young Teruji was put to work in the cane fields.

No more backbreaking work has yet been devised than cane-field labor of that day. So the lad quickly worked his way out of that job to one as fireman of the locomotive which pulled the cane cars. By the time he was nineteen, he'd become an engineer and was casting about for broader horizons.

At twenty he left Kauai and came to Honolulu. Here he signed on as a seaman on an interisland steamer. Like many a seaman before him, he fell in love with a Hawaiian girl on the Big Island and married her in 1923. They stayed there long enough to start a family of three children. Then he brought his brood to Honolulu and got a part-time job as carpenter at Pearl Harbor.

Up to this point, he had settled into the groove of a respectable working man rearing his family in the conventional if not luxurious way. Sumida told me the thought of doing anything illegal never entered his head. Then one day he went to his grocer's to stand off payment of his bill a little longer. The grocer gave him an idea.

"Why don't you go into business?" the grocer asked.

"I don't know anything about business," Sumida protested. "Besides, I don't have any money to start one."

The grocer waved his hand.

"The business I'm talking about you don't need much capital," he said.

"What kind of business is that?"

"Bootlegging."

The Sumida who left the grocery store was a far different man from the Sumida who had entered. As soon as he could learn the ropes, Sumida became a bootlegger and manufactured the powerful native liquor *okolehao,* which sold for a good price during prohibition. Sumida had his first brush with the law in 1930 when he was arrested for bootlegging. He hired a lawyer, beat the case, and continued bootlegging even while the case was pending. How else could he pay his lawyer? he explained.

In 1931 he was nailed again, this time with the "oke" in his car. The result was his first prison term, eighteen months. No sooner was he out than the Feds caught him with the goods again and sent him up for another eighteen months. But he wasn't discouraged. He started retailing the stuff the next time he got out and undoubtedly would have been caught again before long except for the repeal of prohibition.

With his illegal means of livelihood pulled out from under him, Sumida went legitimate. He became a jewelry salesman and a good one. But after years of making easy, illegal money, and having taken a couple of courses from the criminals at Oahu Prison, his income did not satisfy the appetite he had acquired for high living—liquor, good food, and beautiful women. Before long, he was satisfying this appetite with swindles that succeeded because he acted out the fantasy of being a wealthy, retired businessman. He threw lavish parties in various night spots and tipped so generously that his mere presence created a sensation among waitresses, bartenders, and managers.

In fact, he occasionally made spending money by running a small swindle on some restaurant employee. A Japanese bartender admitted that Sumida had taken him for $1,500 cash in a buy-and-sell deal, throughout the whole of which the victim neither saw nor knew anything. Sumida never even told the bartender what business he was in, nor did the bartender inquire. When I asked why he had given Sumida the money, he answered, "I must have been in a trance."

The King of the Fleecers was so smart he made his poor command of English pay dividends. He gave many of his victims the impression he was slightly stupid. Instead of questioning his honesty, they were more likely to be puzzled as to how such a naive, uneducated man could have come by his apparent wealth. They must have reasoned to themselves that, since he was wealthy and not too bright, it couldn't take much brains to be rich if only they got into whatever he was into.

Sumida enlightened them as little as possible. He took $25,000 from one victim in a proposition the man never did understand. When asked what business he was in, Sumida answered mysteriously, "Smart men don't ask questions." The victim eagerly parted with his money.

Another sucker who had been caught well on the hook telephoned the fleecer to come and pick up $15,000 he wanted to invest. Sumida took his own sweet time about coming. When he arrived, the man wrote a check for the amount. Sumida examined the check with care, then looked thoughtfully at the victim.

"You are a smart man," he said. "You know if I go to the bank and cash this check, I got to write my name. They will know you and me are in some funny business."

"I never thought about that," the victim answered. He scurried around to get $15,000 in cash to turn over to Sumida that same afternoon.

The King of the Fleecers worked with simple props. A favorite one-man routine for him ran as follows: He would buy a small piece of candy or bubble gum and wrap it in white paper stuck together with adhesive tape, making it look both secure and unusual. The package went into his watch pocket. Then he put $1,000 in twenty-dollar bills in his wallet and stowed that in his right hip pocket. Another $1,000 in twenties with a hundred-dollar bill outside went into his inside coat pocket.

Thus prepared, he would pick up a sucker in his car and drive to the International Airport, park, and tell his victim to wait in the car while he completed some business. During this conversation,

Sumida would manage to display the $1,000 in his wallet. After a couple of drinks at the airport bar, he'd emerge and show the package from his watch pocket.

"That cost you $1,000?" the sucker would ask incredulously.

"Yes," the fleecer would answer. "But don't worry. I'm going to double my money right now."

With that, he'd drive to Manoa or some other wealthy residential neighborhood, drive slowly past a big house with a doctor's name on it, park some distance away, and walk back out of sight of the sucker. He'd throw the package into a rubbish can and transfer the money from his inside coat pocket to his wallet, showing a total of $2,100. When the sucker saw the total, his eyes usually popped and he was all ready to buy a piece of that or any other deal Sumida had to offer. The fleecer would take the cash and run.

Another favorite build-up was one in which Sumida would borrow and pay back double. A waitress, who had ponied up $12,000 for the fleecer, told us how he would go to the bar where she worked, tip extravagantly, then be caught short and have to borrow amounts beginning at $50 and ranging upward. Each time, he would return the next day to repay the waitress double what he had borrowed. Finally, when her curiosity was sufficiently aroused, he told her he had a big business deal going but not enough cash to carry it through. It would pay 100 percent profit. If she wanted in on a good thing, she'd better raise all the money she could, Sumida told her. The $12,000 she came up with shows how much money waitresses made during World War II.

Besides selling phoney *okolehao* stills, Sumida regularly went in for fake opium deals. Like all confidence games, this swindle requires a mark who has some larceny in his own heart, a desire for easy money and quick profits. In this operation, the mark is allowed to invest a large sum in a highly secret purchase of opium just off the ship. It will be sold immediately at several hundred percent profit.

As a show of good faith, the fleecers allow the mark to accompany them to make a purchase. They indicate that the operation must be carried out with extreme stealth and secrecy, usually in some deserted place and at night. Just after the exchange of money and opium has been made, the "police" show up with flashlights and loud shouts. The mark and the fleecers are lucky to ditch the opium and get away without being arrested. The smuggler has disappeared with the money. If this comes off well, the mark is reluctant about going to the law because he must admit he was willing to enter into an illegal narcotics deal, except that there are no narcotics within miles of this swindle.

As Sumida stayed longer in the fleecing racket, he learned to adapt himself and his ideas to every occasion. He even adapted an old burlesque routine, the one in which a comedian waves a magic pickle under the nose of a beautiful girl and wins her compliance with his will. In this case, the victim was a love-hungry Filipino.

At this time, there were many single Filipinos who had come to our islands to work. Many sought female companionship. Sumida learned that this man wanted a wife. The fleecer ground up some *honohono* grass and squeezed the juice into a cologne bottle. Then he called three of his attractive girl friends and told them it would be to their advantage to meet him that night at a Hotel Street bar.

Sumida then arranged to have the lonely Filipino meet him at the same bar at the same time. The fleecer made sure he and his victim sat at a table next to the three girls, for whom he bought a round of drinks. He asked the Filipino which girl he liked best. The victim picked a *hapa-haole* (half white) girl who got a signal from Sumida. Pretty soon, the girls got up and went to the ladies' room. Sumida then winked at the mark, went over with a show of stealth to the girls' table and poured a few drops from his cologne bottle into the drink of the girl the Filipino had picked.

When the girls came back, the favored one took a sip of her drink, then looked around at the Filipino and smiled at him. Another sip and she became more friendly. After a few more sips, she winked and motioned for the sucker to join her at the table. He was bashful, but the object of his attention more than made up for this deficiency. He got kissed a time or two. The happy couple left the bar together.

Next day the Filipino was back to see Sumida, panting with eagerness. "This one too much good," he enthused. "She speak she love me. Bye and bye, I like marry."

But he was afraid the girl would lose interest in him unless he gave her more of the potion Sumida had poured into her drink. He wanted to buy some. The fleecer hesitated. He explained that it was a dangerous commodity to handle. Besides, he had only one gallon left. The victim was well hooked now. He begged to be allowed to buy that gallon at whatever price the fleecer would name.

The price was $5,000. Sumida told the Filipino to come to a house in a rural suburb of Honolulu the next night and the sale would be made. On the location, he squeezed out some more *honohono* juice, this time into a gallon jug, and mixed it with water. He hid the jug in tall grass by a chicken coop, then tied a cord to the coop and strung it through the grass so he could pull it to make his victim trip.

When the Filipino came, Sumida took his money, warned him to be quiet and careful, and told him where to pick up the jug. From his window he watched to see the man pick up the jug and start back. Then Sumida pulled the end of the cord. The Filipino fell down. There was a sound of breaking glass. The Filipino came running back to the house.

"Boss, boss," he shouted excitedly. "I trip. I fell down. I broke the gallon."

Sumida, afraid the Filipino might want his money back, berated him.

"You lolo! Why you no look where you go? Mo' betta you get outa here quick. Bye and bye policeman come."

The victim departed moaning over his loss of the love potion.

Sumida liked one-man jobs and preferred swindles in which he used little except the aura of money, mystery, and influence he built around himself. But he was capable of setting up elaborate situations, too, and working with several confederates when necessary. No swindle was more intricate than the one he pulled on a Honolulu fireman and his wife, a couple thrifty and foresighted enough to acquire four houses and some capital.

The unusual feature of this hoax was that Sumida used a *kahuna* (Hawaiian priest), considered in the public mind as a sort of witch doctor or medicine man. He is supposed to have mysterious powers of both good and evil, but mostly the ones you hear about are those of evil. A number of people, especially Hawaiians, believe in the powers of *kahunas*. As recently as 1953, a federal judge said he was told a *kahuna* had put a spell on him following his decision in a much-publicized trial.

Sumida knew a *kahuna* who knew the fireman and his wife, so the master fleecer worked out a plot to fit the situation. First, he promised the *kahuna* a share of the profits for playing along. He had the *kahuna* tell the fireman and his wife a sad story about a wealthy jeweler, a friend of the *kahuna*, who would shortly arrive from the island of Hawaii. The wealthy man's wife had run off with a soldier (no incredible story during World War II) and had left the jeweler bereaved, though wallowing in wealth, and in charge of the four children his wife had left behind. Now the jeweler was coming to Honolulu in search of his wife and to make a reconciliation if he could find her. The *kahuna* was going to help as best he might. And the "wealthy jeweler," of course, was Sumida himself.

The victims, a warm-hearted couple, offered to play hosts to the unhappy man. When he arrived, they installed him in their home. He retold the story, with tears streaming down his face, describing how the children cried for their absent mother. Now he had taken the last desperate step to bring his wife back. He had employed a *kahuna*.

Sumida became the honored guest of the home while the *kahuna* supposedly set about his mysterious machinations. The fleecer slept in the master bedroom, took his meals at the house, drank the liquor of his hosts, and was given the use of their car. From time to time, the *kahuna* would perform a ritual before all present, using a glass of water and his mysterious knowledge to inform Sumida of the doings between his imaginary wife and the soldier. In this way, they all learned that the wife was staying at an Army post in Honolulu with the soldier and that she was very unhappy. Meanwhile, the *kahuna* described in casual conversation with the fireman and his wife the wealth and business connections of their guest.

Soon the victims were emotionally involved in Sumida's marital problem and were sympathizing with him. Naturally, he couldn't be worrying about his wife all the time. During periods of relaxation he described his jewelry business, the largest in Hilo, and the building he expected to erect soon in Waikiki, a very large building. It would include a jewelry shop.

After he became better acquainted with the fireman and his wife, Sumida admitted that he would need investors. The fireman's wife expressed interest. Sumida mentioned off-hand that she and her husband would realize from 30 to 40 percent profit easily if they had a bit of capital to put up. The woman's eyes got as big as two eggs sunny-side up at this information, but she said she would have to talk to her husband.

At this critical juncture, the *kahuna* announced at a rite with the fireman and his wife present that the erring wife would leave the soldier the next day and visit the house. Sumida then borrowed his victim's car and drove to a bar downtown where he knew a waitress. He told her she could make a couple hundred dollars if she would play the part of his wife the next day. She jumped at the chance.

The next day the girl got out of a taxi about a block away from the house and walked slowly up the street looking at each house. When she came to the house where the swindler was sitting on the front porch with the fireman's wife, she ran up and embraced him. The fireman came out to see what was happening. Sumida and the girl embraced with even more emotion, weeping over one another. The victims tactfully but firmly ordered the swindler and his "wife" into the bedroom. They emerged half an hour later in a state of bliss. Sumida, or Yamamoto as he was calling himself, peeled $200 off his roll and gave it to the girl, then told a confederate to drive her to the airport so that she could get back to the children on Hawaii as soon as possible.

He explained to the fireman and his wife that he would follow in a day or so, as soon as he wound up certain business affairs. Taking their cue, the fireman and his wife mortgaged their four houses and on the second day, produced $14,000 which they now wished to invest in the jewelry business. Sumida suggested that they might be able to borrow another $1,000 or $1,500 on their car. Fortunately for them, they felt they were in deep enough already.

He then took leave of the couple midst fond goodbyes and, so far as they knew, headed back to Hilo. They never saw him again. Growing suspicious, they hired a private detective but had no luck finding the fleecer. After a month, the fireman's wife went to Hilo herself. She discovered that no jeweler there had ever heard of Alexander Yamamoto. In the end, the couple had to sell one of their four houses to pay the interest and mortgage on the other three.

Once Sumida had found his niche in the criminal world, one which kept him safe from the law, it is surprising that he ever left it. Possibly the initiative of the man inspired him to set up at least one job of robbery. A fingerman told him of a mark who had $24,000 in cash in his house. Sumida got in touch with the man. His story was that he had a number of one-hundred-dollar bills he couldn't cash in Hawaii because they had been used as occupation money during World War II. Sumida needed cash, so he would sell each $100 bill for $80 to the man, who could later cash them on the mainland. The mark fell for this proposition. Arrangements were made for them to meet at the victim's house the next day.

In the meantime, Sumida hired a young white man, recently discharged from the service, to appear at the proper time and pose as a Los Angeles policeman. The fleecer entered the victim's house carrying only a roll with three one-hundred-dollar bills and a ten-dollar bill underneath. But, with his smooth line of patter, he soon had the victim displaying his $24,000 on the living-room table. At this point, the bogus cop walked in and arrested Sumida, telling him he was wanted for questioning in Los Angeles. The phony cop scooped up the two packages of money on the table as evidence. Once outside, the "cop" and Sumida sped off in a car.

They drove to College Walk where Sumida got out, paid off his accomplice with $1,000 and the driver with a cut, then took a cab back into the middle of the business section of town. There he changed cabs and went to his apartment, where he hid most of the money. Then he took still another cab to a downtown hotel, rented a room, and went to bed. There he was awakened and arrested by

143

police (the real thing this time) who took $1,000 from him and accused him of robbery. Sumida feigned innocence. The bogus cop was picked up the next day and both were charged with conspiracy to rob. While his case was pending, Sumida wrote letters to the court and the prosecutor's office denying the robbery and demanding that the police return the $1,000 (which he had swindled).

Yet, it wasn't this slip-up which caused the swindler's downfall. That was achieved by one of his suckers who employed means that would make the average fleecer laugh. This victim, knowing he had no recourse through criminal law, sued the swindler in civil court for the $25,000 he said Sumida had taken from him in a bogus diamond deal.

Sumida had a perfect defense. He said there had never been any talk of bogus diamonds. What they had talked about was narcotics and a deal had been made. But he hadn't fleeced anyone. He'd been ready to sell the narcotics as he promised. With righteous indignation, the swindler said he had grown tired of all this talk about diamonds. "I cannot stand it any longer," he said. With that, he banged a number of morphine Syrettes on the table to be introduced into the case as evidence. He said it was part of the narcotics shipment he was selling to the complainant.

Sumida's dramatic defense caused a bigger sensation in court than he expected. He won the case. But federal agents put the arm on him as he left the courtroom and charged him with illegal possession of narcotics. This time he couldn't squirm out of it. He got four years, and at his age, fifty-nine, it was more than he could face. That was on May 31, 1950.

On April 17, 1951, the telephone rang in the office of City and County Prosecutor Allen Hawkins. When Mr. Hawkins picked up the phone, a voice said, "This is Alex."

"Alex who?" asked Mr. Hawkins.

"Alex Sumida."

"Yes Alex?"

"I want to talk."

"Talk about what, Alex?"

"I want tell everything about all the jobs I been do."

Hawkins set a date to hear Alex Sumida sing and hung up. Val

Cederlof and I were in the prosecutor's office at the time on other business. Mr. Hawkins grinned broadly and Val chuckled a little. I wondered if it was another of Sumida's well-planned swindles.

Quite an impressive array faced the aging fleecer in the prison boardroom a couple of days later. The crowd included Mr. Hawkins, Police Chief Dan Liu, Captain Arthur Tarbell, Sergeant Shigeru Kabei, Val Cederlof, and me. Sumida began like a lecturer and, considering his poor command of the English language, he did pretty well. He came to the point quickly. As I had suspected, he wanted something.

"My mother die Hiroshima when I small boy," he said. "I want go back to see her grave before I die. I very sick man. I diabetic. I work in hospital so I can be close to medical attention."

Well, his bargain was in the open. But we were in no position to meet it and I told him so. We could offer no immunity for anything he might say. Besides, he was a federal prisoner and so we had no control over his case. If he was going to talk, it would have to be of his own volition without hope of any deal.

"No, no," he protested quickly. "I not asking you make promises. All I telling you, when I get out, I want go back Japan."

Hawkins and Chief Dan Liu told him they believed that when the right time came, the U.S. Immigration Service would see that his request was granted. We knew he was an alien subject to deportation on release from prison. He probably knew it, too. He was just speeding up that release a little by talking.

With these preliminaries over, his story unfolded. I have to say it checked in every detail that could be checked. After he finished with us, he sold a lot of his stories to *The Advertiser,* which ran a serialized version of his life. From then on, he had to be protected from the other prison inmates who were ready to kill him for squealing. That worried the old fleecer less than not getting on the front page.

At the end of his long recitals, which included confession to fifty-three fleecing cases, a couple of burglaries, one taxi robbery, and other peccadillos, in total accounting for $256,710 worth of fleecing and $24,000 in the robbery, Sumida took another step in his new role of law-abiding citizen. He had the nerve to make a complaint against the person or persons who had broken into his Waikiki hotel room back in 1948 and robbed him of $4,300.

Meanwhile, he got what he had been hoping for. On October 31, 1953, Governor Samuel Wilder King granted him executive clemency on condition that he leave the country. Val and Lieutenant Albert Fraga and I went to the immigration station to bid him bon voyage. He hinted around about a big sucker he could take if we'd just give him a week off. But we didn't fall for that.

He sent Val a card from Japan immediately upon landing. That was all. The next we heard of him was a story in the local news about how he had been arrested in Yokohama on charges of passing $500 worth of bad checks. Yokohama police said he looked like a vagrant when he was picked up. He boasted to his jailers about his long and successful career as a fleecer and said he was going to write a book. I doubt if he meant it. Sumida died in bed in the prison hospital on May 8, 1954. All the money he had was twenty-eight cents they took from him when he entered the jail.

What might the man have accomplished if his parents had sent him to school when he was a boy, as he had wished? Would he have turned to a legitimate business and prospered? Or would he have become an even more adept fleecer? I've never been able even to guess at the answer.

17

The Unsolved Murder

A LOT of the investigating that Val and I did now was with unsolved crimes, cases that had lain in the police files for years. We cleaned up quite a few old cases at the request of Chief Dan Liu. One is still on the books through no fault of our own. It still burns me up.

We got the case of Matsusuke Takara, the headwaiter who never got home, seventeen years after it happened. As usual, there were a lot of musty old files to go through. We made an early decision to forget about Takara's premonitions of death and stories about *haole*s in dark suits on the night of the murder, and tried to find the local girl friends of those Fort Ruger soldiers whom the police had questioned.

One of them, a waitress, had told police about two soldiers who had come to the sandwich shop on John Ena Road where she worked after midnight on March 1. She had said one of the soldiers was wearing an aloha shirt and that his face was covered with blood and dirt. When she had asked him what happened, he had said he was in a fight.

That didn't fit with the story the soldier had told police about falling down and hitting his head. But the police hadn't followed up on it. So we put out our feelers, and in a week or so, Jane Kealoha came tripping into our office at City Hall. It didn't take too much persuasion to get her to talk about her flaming youth when she'd been seventeen years old and most of her boy friends had been soldiers of the old Army.

One reason she talked freely was because the soldiers involved were long since gone from the Territory. She said she had been afraid of them. Because of that fear, she had never told the whole truth to the detectives back in 1938. Ever since, the murder of Matsusuke Takara had weighed on her mind. Now she was a married woman with a child. She said the prospect of reliving her youth in a courtroom was anything but pleasant, but the desire to clear her conscience was stronger.

We knew immediately we'd struck pay dirt. She went over her earlier story to the police—how the soldier Minolek had explained his bruises, not by a fall to the ground but by saying he'd had a fight with a gook back at the Rendezvous Dance Hall. She told again about the wristwatch she had loaned him, the watch with a broken crystal and broken link strap, the link strap that matched marks made on the victim's throat.

Only this time, the witness added details she had not told police. Earlier, she had described her ride in the soldiers' cars in a way that gave them an alibi—that the route they had taken avoided McCully Street in the section where Takara's body was found. Now she said this was a lie, that the route had actually been by McCully Street, and that the soldiers had told her what to tell police.

With this witness to back it up, our other evidence fell into place. We felt we had enough to go to the grand jury. But first we had to locate the soldiers Minolek and Mearns. Two decades had passed. We didn't know where they were living or even whether they were still alive. So we started digging again.

From police arrest records, we learned the cities and states where Minolek and Mearns had enlisted from; we also looked into the other two soldiers, Boise and Jeeter, who had been along that night and might figure as material witnesses. At our request, Chief Dan Liu sent photographs of the four along with letters asking chiefs of police and sheriffs where we thought the suspects might be located to make discreet inquiries. In due course, we had located Minolek in Texas, Mearns in Michigan, the other two in Georgia and California.

The next move was up to us. By April 21, we had eighteen witnesses subpoenaed to testify before the grand jury. Then, to our amazement, the prosecutor asked for a continuance. The performance was repeated over a period of months. The grand jury even inquired about the case, indicating it was ready to bring in a true bill. The prosecutor still stalled.

He told us in private that he felt Val and I should make a trip to the mainland to question the soldiers before asking for an indictment. We refused to make the trip without indictments in our pockets. The deadlock continued until that term of the grand jury ended.

Meanwhile, Val and I put our evidence together and gave it to Chief Liu. He sent the information out to see if police in Texas and Michigan could get confessions. The captain of detectives in a Texas city said he couldn't get a confession, but the reaction was so hot that he was convinced we had the right man. In Michigan, Georgia, and California, there wasn't much to report.

The case ended there for Val and me. All our work went for nothing. It is some consolation to remember that there are five penalties for the crime of homicide in Hawaii. Three are life imprisonment without parole, twenty years, or ten years in prison. A fourth is the killer's own conscience. The fifth comes when he is called before his god for judgment. The killer, or killers, of Matsusuke Takara will one day know which of the five is the greatest punishment.

18

A Confession after Twenty-Two Years

THE longer you work as a detective, the less you are surprised at the variety of situations that can produce evidence in a murder case. It was a random conversation in May of 1953 that sent Val Cederlof and me down into the basement of City Hall to dust the cobwebs off a stack of yellowing reports twenty-two years old. For me, that was the beginning of an investigation which resulted in the most poignant tragedy with which I was ever connected.

Those reports were typed on an old Police Department Underwood. They said that on March 7, 1931, Fire Lieutenant John Kanae Anderson, answering an alarm from the Enos Lane area, detected smoke coming from one of the cottages on the lane. He kicked the door open. It was dark except for a slow fire smouldering around a bed upon which lay the body of a man. Anderson's crew quickly extinguished the fire.

The body was partially charred and the mattress badly burned. Otherwise, the house suffered little damage. There was a strong smell of kerosene in the air. The firemen found a half-empty gallon jug of kerosene in the kitchen. Among the other items listed on the premises were two hammers. The circumstances didn't arouse the lieutenant's suspicions at the moment, although they struck him as a little peculiar.

Fire Chief Wallace Blaisdell, who answered many alarms personally in the manner traditional with Honolulu fire chiefs, also noticed a couple of peculiar things that didn't come out until later. For one thing, bodies of persons who meet death by fire are usually swollen. This one wasn't. Still, the experienced fire chief didn't consider the possibility of foul play. He just made a routine report to the police and stated that a man's body had been found at the scene of the fire.

The coroner's examination of the body was just as routinely conducted. Robert Loo, son of the dead man, arrived from downtown Honolulu where he had spent the evening. He identified the body of his father, Patrick Pang Loo, forty-four years old, and offered the opinion that he might have been smoking in bed, which could have set the fire and burned him to death.

Young Loo went home. Some time after midnight, the telephone rang. He answered it. The caller was Frances Hong, a friend of the dead man. She asked, "How is papa?" Young Loo told her his father had been burned to death in a fire. She expressed shock and sorrow and hung up.

The routine continued the next day with the coroner calling Silva's Mortuary to say Pang Loo's family wanted them to take charge of the body. Embalmer Manuel Silva Barros came over for it. He learned that it had been Pang Loo's desire to be cremated. The coroner told Barros to take the body to the City and County emergency hospital for a death certificate before taking it to the mortuary.

About that time, Barros noticed a few things nobody else had. When the body was lifted from the bed, he saw blood on the side of the head that had been against the mattress. Then he saw cuts on the forehead. He pointed these out to Dr. David Liu who examined the body at the emergency hospital. Liu told Barros to take the body along and he would issue a death certificate in the morning. Had that happened, the death of Patrick Pang Loo would have been attributed to his careless handling of cigarets.

But by the following morning, Dr. Liu began having second thoughts. When the mortuary called for a death certificate, he told them to take the body to the morgue of the Territorial Board of Health. Dr. Robert Faus, the city physician, wanted to perform an autopsy. That autopsy revealed a cause of death quite different from burning. Semicircular lacerations on the forehead and temples were identical to those caused by hammer blows. One of those blows had penetrated deeply enough to lacerate the brain and cause death. It was a clear case of homicide.

151

Val Cederlof, then a police detective working out of headquarters, took young Robert Loo into custody on suspicion of killing his father. As it turned out, the son had an excellent alibi for the time of the murder. He'd been shooting pool in a billiard parlor on Bethel Street in downtown Honolulu when it happened. In fact, he had been shooting pool there nearly every Saturday night for several years.

Loo told Cederlof that his father didn't want him around the house on Saturday nights. Those were nights of romance for the father and a woman who had visited him at his home for a number of years. Loo said his mother was still living but that she was blind and living on the island of Kauai with relatives. The father had taken pains to keep the affair from his son, but young Loo knew about it anyway. The woman was married, mother of several children, and living with her husband and family. Then it came out that her name was Frances Hong. She was the one who had called him on the night of the fire. She had also been in communication with him later to warn him not to tell anyone about the affair.

The investigation picked up momentum after that. Val took Frances Hong into custody. Then they located a taxi driver who knew almost as much about the romance as the middle-aged lovers. He was Tomito Imahiro who had brought Frances Hong to the Loo house every Saturday night since the beginning of the affair, five or six years before, then called to take her back to a corner from where she walked to her home in Waikiki.

From these witnesses, police detectives fitted together a picture of the romance that was not all sunshine and roses. Young Loo said he had heard his father arguing violently with Frances from time to time. He didn't know what it was all about because they spoke Chinese, which he knew only a smattering of. The taxi driver made the same observation, though he couldn't understand Chinese either. He didn't have to when Frances began asking whether or not he had brought other girls, Chinese girls, to see Pang Loo. Once she confessed to Imahiro that she was sick with jealousy. She had asked again about other girls a week before the fire.

Describing the night of the murder, Imahiro said he got a call from Pang Loo on Saturday afternoon saying he wanted to be picked up at 7:15 P.M. on Enos Lane and Makiki Street. Pang Loo got in the front seat with the driver who, in conversation that followed, said he had heard arguments between the pair.

"She is very jealous," said Pang Loo. "So jealous she makes me sick."

The two men drove to the meeting spot in Waikiki, John Ena Road and Kalakaua Avenue, where Frances was waiting. She got in the back seat and Pang Loo moved back with her. As usual, they drove to Pang Loo's house. The taxi driver said Pang Loo was surprised and irritated to find that his son hadn't left the house. Frances stayed in the taxi while Loo went inside. Imahiro said he heard Loo cussing his son out, asking, "What the hell are you doing here?" Almost immediately, Robert left the house and Frances went in. Young Loo told Imahiro to bring the taxi back at 10 P.M. and take Frances home, then left.

But it didn't work out that way. About 8:30 P.M. Frances called Imahiro at his taxi stand to come and pick her up. Before he could leave, the phone rang. It was Frances again. This time she told him not to come right away. She'd call later. Shortly after nine o'clock, she called once more, and Imahiro, whose entire Saturday night business seemed connected with Pang Loo's love life, took off again to pick her up.

When he got there, he remained outside the lane as instructed. Presently Frances came out. Imahiro recalled that she wore a black cape that night. He also remembered something a little unusual. Pang Loo didn't come to the door to tell her good-bye, a courtesy common among Chinese. The taxi driver figured the lovers had been fighting again.

"What's the matter with Loo tonight? No go?" he asked.

"No," Frances answered. "Take me home."

Imahiro backed his taxi out of the lane and into Makiki Street. He had turned and was heading away when Frances changed her mind again.

"Take me back," she said.

The taxi driver turned around, dropped her off across from the entry of the lane, and waited. Frances went through the entry but it was dark, so Imahiro couldn't see where she went after that.

153

When she came out a few minutes later, he asked, "What's the matter?"

"Mr. Loo is sick," Frances answered.

This puzzled the taxi driver because Loo had been hearty and healthy earlier in the evening. Something else seemed odd. It was the first time since he had been driving for the lovers that he had taken Frances home alone as early as that.

Two days later, on March 9, the morning the result of the autopsy came out, she visited him at his taxi stand to ask if he'd heard what happened to Pang Loo. Imahiro said he had. Frances asked what time he had brought her home that night. He told her it was 9:20 P.M. when they left Enos Lane and 9:30 when he dropped her off. Frances explained that she had been worried about Loo's illness. That's why she went back, to put a hot water bottle on him.

"That was very kind," Imahiro commented.

"It is best we don't know anything about this trouble," she said to the taxi driver. "We tell them [the police] we don't know anything."

By this time, evidence was piling pretty high around Frances. The police never did find any hot water bottle anywhere on the premises. Two junior high school girls who lived across Enos Lane remembered hearing a strange cry they felt might have indicated pain and surprise coming from the bedroom of Loo's house sometime after 7:30 on the night of the murder. They said it was the voice of their neighbor, Patrick Pang Loo. There was no evidence that anybody had been in the house but Loo and Frances Hong.

But where was the hammer, if that's what it was, that inflicted the death wound? Firemen had found two hammers. But Robert Loo described another, with tape on the handle, property of the landlord. That was missing. Was it the murder weapon?

Meanwhile, the police got Frances' story. She admitted that she had carried on an affair with the dead man. She intimated that, if it hadn't been for the interference of her mother years ago, she might have been Loo's wife instead of being married to the man who was only now learning of his wife's infidelity; and her four children would not now be put in such a position of public embarrassment. At age fourteen, in love with Pang Loo, she was pushed into matrimony with another man because her mother insisted Loo was no good. Frances said no one knew about the affair except Robert, and they had tried to keep it from him as much as possible.

Frances said she had been faithful to Pang Loo in spite of the fact that he had made a pretty, young Chinese girl pregnant. She had even gone to Loo and tried to get him to have a doctor fix up the girl. But by then it was too late. So Frances told the girl to keep the baby when it was born and she, Frances, would have it adopted. Apparently she had asked the taxi driver about other girls. He, being discreet, said he didn't know of any.

Then she told about the fatal night. She said she had come to the house with Loo in Imahiro's taxi. When Robert left the house after being scolded by his father, she had scrunched down in the back seat and was confident he hadn't seen her. Inside the house, she and Loo had undressed and gone to bed. For some time they had lain there talking and arguing. The argument, according to Frances, was largely an academic one from her point of view. Loo had pondered the recent death of his father, a suicide. Loo had said hotly that his mother had virtually forced his father to take poison. Frances, who had loaned Loo $150 to bury his father, argued that his mother was really a good woman. The argument had grown somewhat heated, then subsided. There had been no violence of any kind, she said.

One of the officers asked, "Was that the time when somebody went into the kitchen and somebody came back and struck him in the head?"

"No, not that time," Frances answered.

The question wasn't followed up. Instead, Frances was asked if she had murdered Loo.

"How can I do that? I love him so much," she answered.

"But he was murdered," the officer insisted.

"No. His son Robert told me he was burned in the house when it caught on fire."

Going on with her story, Frances said she and Loo had lain in bed for about an hour when he complained of feeling ill and chilly.

He asked her to give him a rubdown. She said she had gone to the kitchen to get some peanut oil and did rub him down. By that time she was feeling ill, so she told Loo it would be better for her to go home. She explained her delay of the taxi, after calling, to give her time to make Loo more comfortable. Then she had asked to be taken back to ask how he was and to promise that she would send a hot water bottle from home. But she forgot.

If that was a feeble attempt at an alibi, it didn't impress Cederlof and the other detectives much. Still, they checked out other persons with a possible motive for murdering Loo. There was Frances' husband, Hong. Could he have found out about the affair without her knowledge and killed Loo in such a way as to make Frances look responsible? There was the family of the pretty, young Chinese girl whom Loo had made pregnant. Might one of them have avenged the girl's honor that night in Enos Lane? And there was Robert. Did he resent his father enough to take a hammer to him? These possibilities were all chased down by police. Every one ran into a dead end.

Frances Hong was charged with the first-degree murder of Patrick Pang Loo on March 10, 1931, and was bound over for the grand jury. The police were proud of their efficient investigation. But the grand jury didn't see it that way. They refused to indict. Within a month after she had been charged, Frances was turned loose.

The murder remained unsolved for twenty-two years. Then one day in 1953, some new witnesses turned up in the most unlikely place, right in our own office. The witnesses were my bosses, Chief Public Prosecutor Robert St. Sure and his brother, Assistant Deputy Prosecutor George St. Sure. For some reason, the Patrick Pang Loo murder came up in conversation. They remembered it for a very good reason. They had been students at the University of Hawaii at the time. It turned out they'd been sitting in a car out on Enos Lane, waiting for a friend living in a nearby residence, when a woman came out of Patrick Pang Loo's house, passed their car, and entered a taxi parked on Makiki Street outside the entrance of the lane. They remembered that she wore a black cloak, that she appeared to be in a hurry, and that she seemed to have trouble with her feet. Later, they saw the activity at Pang Loo's home and heard of the fire and his death. They had never told anyone about the woman in the night until now.

After that conversation, Investigator Alfred Souza and I did some checking. We found that Frances was still alive though her husband had passed on. She was sixty-one and living in Kaimuki. My notes show that it was 2:05 P.M. on June 1, 1953, when Val Cederlof, Souza, Policewoman Momi Lum, and I arrived at the house where Mrs. Hong lived. Cederlof and I waited in the car while Souza and Momi Lum went to the door and called for Frances. They told her there were some questions we wanted to ask on an old case. She came voluntarily.

As she approached the car, I got my first look at her. Even at sixty-one, she was an attractive woman. There was some gray in her hair but she was far younger-looking than I had expected. We did not put her under arrest.

The four of us began questioning her in one of the side rooms of our office. She told us of her birth on Maui, her early life there, coming to Honolulu with her parents, how she got work as a sort of babysitter until she met Hong and married. She also told us of her youthful romance with Patrick Pang Loo and its obstacle, her mother. Frances said she started seeing Loo again some time in 1924. Then she clammed up.

"I'm not making any more statements," she said suddenly. "If you want to find out what I did, you go see the statements I made before."

We began to bring a little pressure to bear. I told her of the new evidence, of eyewitnesses who had seen her leave the house. I said we had corroboration by two junior high school girls who were now grown women. The fact was, we had little more evidence than the police had had twenty-two years before. But Frances didn't know that. When I saw that she was considering her new peril, I appealed to her conscience. Then, after more than two hours of questioning, we left her alone with Momi Lum. It was Momi, daughter of a veteran Honolulu police officer, Dewey O. Mookini, who was the first to hear Frances confess she had killed Patrick Pang Loo twenty-two years before.

157

Momi came out of the office after half an hour and told me Frances had given a partial, oral confession. She had further consented to confess to me, along with Momi. But she wouldn't let Cederlof or Souza sit in. For some reason, she didn't like them. Frances began talking. I took down what she said. But she grew more distraught by the moment. When I showed her what I had written, she tore it up. Momi and I pieced the fragments together. Here is what the first confession said:

"I have children. I am so ashamed. I killed a man. I feel sorry for my children. I killed him but there was no reason. He owed me $150 I loaned him, but I forget when. Look at my [bank] statement. I withdrew the $150 from the Bank of Hawaii. The money in the bank was in my name. I gave him the money at his house."

Momi and I began questioning her again, confronting her with the confession we had pieced together. Fifteen minutes later, we began taking a second confession. This one Frances didn't tear up after it was finished. She said she had gone to the house that night twenty-two years before, hoping to collect the $150.

Her confession read: "He told me he was not going to pay me and he was never going to pay me. He pushed me and told me to get the hell out of there. I looked for the hammer and found it in the house. I don't know if it was in the kitchen or where. Then I went back in the bedroom and struck him on the head. I don't know how many times I struck him. He was sitting on a chair near the bed when I hit him. He fell on the bed and straightened himself out. . . ."

Then, Frances said, she got panicky. Her rage was gone and she suddenly realized she had committed murder. What was she to do? She called the taxi driver, then called back and told him not to come. For a time, she just sat in the living room and wept. The next time she called the taxi, she left the house. But she returned to the house once. She said she thought of calling the police then and giving up. Then she changed her mind again and left.

Frances didn't confess to setting the house on fire. Again, she tried to clamp down on the flow of thoughts and words that had been dammed up inside her for twenty-two years. The end of her confession reads: "That is all I am going to tell you. I am not going to tell any more. My children are big. All this publicity. They will know I'm a murderer. All my friends will hate me. I'm going to be a Catholic. I am going to be baptized and pray to God."

When she finished her confession, some of the tension seemed to leave her. She talked more easily. She repeated that she had been a Buddhist but that she was going to become a Catholic and pray to God for forgiveness.

"I'm glad you feel that way," I told her. "I'm a Catholic. I've been a Catholic since I was a little boy."

Frances seemed to see me in a new light. She smiled and extended her hand. I shook it.

The scene may have seemed strange to anyone but a detective. I had just been a party to inducing Frances Hong to confessing the most serious crime there is. Through my words and actions, she had placed herself in a position where she knew she would have to pay the penalty. You might have expected her to hate me, to spit at me and claw my face. There are some who react that way. But there are many others who react somewhat as Frances did.

For a moment there was a strange sort of emotional bond between me, the hunter, and Frances, the hunted, finally captured with defenses destroyed. It was a sort of friendliness and something perhaps a little deeper. After all, I had just helped induce her to bare her most intimate experience. So now she shook my hand and smiled. I smiled back and told her she looked young and attractive for her age. For the moment, she looked as though she might have won a prize at a social club instead of having just confessed to a murder.

Then the mood changed to another that surprised even me. She said she ought to be getting home now. She had to cook some rice for a boy who lived with her. Then too, she wanted to talk over the case with her oldest daughter. It was as if she'd had a real nice little visit with us and was making polite excuses for leaving. I couldn't help wondering if she realized yet what her confession meant. Her mention of talking over the case had come second to her obligation to cook the rice. Did she understand that, in the years to come, she

159

would not be cooking rice for anybody? Then some of that realization seemed to come back to her. She said she'd be back with her oldest daughter the following morning.

I could have taken her into custody immediately, of course. Some police officials think I should have. But I believe that police work, even the apprehension of murderers, should be done as humanely as possible. Frances Hong seemed composed after her confession and dedicated to seeking forgiveness for her crime. Besides, what chance did she have to escape here in the islands? We took her home.

The next morning, when Alfred Souza and Momi Lum rang the bell at Frances' house in Kaimuki, they raised no one at all. They came back to where Val and I were waiting in the car. Wondering what had happened, Momi Lum went to the house of a neighbor and made a phone call to Mrs. Hong's house. There was no answer.

We called back to our office but Frances Hong hadn't shown up there. After waiting an hour, we visited the eldest daughter in another part of town. She told us some fast activity had gone on the night before. Frances Hong had called her daughter after leaving our office and had taken her to visit a Chinese woman who owed Frances some money. In the presence of her daughter, Frances got the woman to agree that the debt should be paid to the daughter. Mother and daughter then went to the house in Kaimuki. Frances gave her daughter some sugar and coffee, and told her to go home, her husband was waiting for her.

Noon went by. There wasn't much we could do but wait. About 3 P.M., while we were sitting in Momi Lum's car wondering what to do next, an "8,000" police call came over the radio. That's a suicide. Momi Lum called in to ask whether it was a male or female. She was told it was a male.

Then we got a lead. We learned from a neighbor that Frances had left home in a taxi the night before and had never returned. We called the owner of the taxi. He told of a driver, now off duty, who had picked up a Chinese lady and taken her to the vicinity of Hanauma Bay, a resort beach some ten miles from Honolulu. The beach is in an extinct volcanic crater which has high cliffs on three sides. At that time, no one went there at night except flirtatious couples seeking seclusion.

The passenger in this case hadn't even known where the bay was. When the driver passed Diamond Head, she asked if they had arrived at Hanauma Bay. He told her it was much farther on. His fare got out on arrival at the entrance to the bay and began walking quietly in the dark. He waited, puzzled by her behavior, until she told him she was expecting someone and urged him to go away. He drove back to the taxi stand and told his boss what had happened.

After hearing this story, Momi Lum called the Detective Division again. This time she learned that the body of the suicide was a woman, not a man. The woman had been identified as Frances Hong. There were even witnesses to the suicide. Late the night before, two men in the area using a spotlight had turned it on the cliffs above the Blow Hole, a tourist attraction near the bay. They saw a woman standing poised for a leap. They tried to shout her down. The attention seemed to strengthen her resolution. They saw her jump to her death on the rocks and in the sea below. As nearly as we could reconstruct what happened, Frances had sat near the Blow Hole from 9 P.M. to 1:30 A.M. Then she had determined to take her own life.

A lot of people have asked me how Frances Hong got the chance to commit suicide; why I didn't take her into custody as soon as she confessed. There are police officers who think I made a mistake in judgment. I have thought it over many times since, and I still don't think I was wrong. These are my reasons:

She had given no indication of wanting to destroy herself. Instead, she gave every sign of repentance. She wanted to break the news to her family in her own way and settle her affairs. She had been a Buddhist and she wanted to join the Catholic Church and pray to God for forgiveness. I believed she should have what she asked for, one last night before she went to jail and before the whole community knew her story. I will go to my grave believing she was honest with me at the time she promised to return to our office the next morning.

I also think she hadn't then realized the full implications of her confession. The whole impact of what had happened must have sunk in later. When she realized that soon all the people she had known would know about her crime and its motive, she knew it was a situation she could not face. Frances had been strong enough to bear the burden of her crime in secret for twenty-two years. But she was now too weak to face the consequences. Or perhaps she was strong. She acted as her own judge and jury and, having passed sentence on herself, was her own executioner. The thought of the terrible pressure that Frances Hong endured for twenty-two years, only to feel she was forced in the end to take her own life, leaves me stupefied.

But the job of a police detective is to find the killer, not to worry about the pressures that help in the capture. If I didn't believe that, I would not be able to do my job.

John Jardine joined the Honolulu Police Department on July 16, 1923. He is shown here a rookie cop in his new uniform. He patroled beats in some of the town's toughest areas, including Hell's Half Acre and Tin Can Alley, as well as Aala Park. *Photo courtesy of Mrs. John Jardine*

John Troche *(center)* joined the police force before Jardine did and rose through the ranks to the Detective Division. Troche and Jardine solved many cases together. In this photo taken in the 1920s Troche is standing between the paddy wagon Black Maria and the police ambulance. *Photo courtesy of Mrs. John Jardine*

John Jardine and Val Cederlof became two of Honolulu's most respected detectives as special investigators for the public prosecutor's office from the 1930s into the 1960s. The team became known for solving cases long forgotten. One crime that was committed in 1931, for example, was solved in 1953. Jardine and Cederlof also broke the police graft case of 1946. The Honolulu Advertiser *photo*

Chief of Police William A. Gabrielson took over the department on August 8, 1932, after it was reorganized as a result of the Massie case. He resigned on April 12, 1946, during the police graft scandal which Jardine and his partner, Val Cederlof, investigated. *State Archives photo from the Abel Fraga collection*

Patrick Gleason was the last sheriff in charge of the Honolulu Police Department. Backlash from the Massie case created demands for reform in 1932. An appointed police chief replaced the elected sheriff. Jardine thought Gleason a conscientious official and a hard worker. *State Archives photo from the Abel Fraga collection*

John Kelley, public prosecutor, picked John Jardine from the Detective Division of the Police Department and put him to work as a special investigator on April 6, 1936. From that time on Jardine worked on special assignments or on cases that police detectives had not solved. *Photo courtesy of Mrs. John Jardine*

Sergeant Henry A. Chillingworth working in the radio dispatch room of the police station in 1934, while Sergeant Oliver Barboza checks his records. Chillingworth was murdered two years later. Jardine solved the case. *State Archives photo from the Abel Fraga collection*

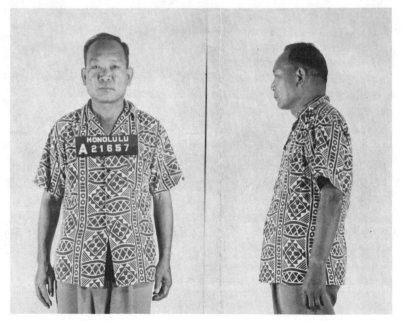

Alex Sumida, known in the 1940s and the 1950s as the King of the Fleecers, was one of Hawaii's most colorful criminals. Jardine, who took his confession, said few confidence men could match him. The Honolulu Advertiser *photo*

Thalia and Lieutenant Thomas Massie a few days after she had reported being driven in a touring car to an isolated spot where she was raped by local youths. Jardine was on duty that night. He investigated the case which became one of the most famous crimes in Hawaii's history. Honolulu Star-Bulletin *photo*

Five local youths were charged with the rape of Thalia Massie, wife of Navy Lieutenant Thomas Massie, on September 12, 1931. They were tried and found not guilty. *Left to right, top row:* David Takai, Horace Ida, and Henry Chang. *Bottom row:* Benny Ahakuelo and Joe Kahahawai. Honolulu Star-Bulletin *photo*

The Massie case became a national sensation when Lieutenant Thomas Massie and Mrs. Granville Roland Fortescue, his mother-in-law, were convicted of murdering Joe Kahahawai, one of Thalia Massie's alleged attackers. Clarence Darrow, famous defense attorney, came out of retirement to take the case. They are shown here leaving the courthouse. Governor Lawrence Judd commuted the sentences of Massie and Fortescue. Honolulu Star-Bulletin *photo*

The touring car driven by Horace Ida. It figured heavily in the Massie case, as its license number, 58-895, became a controversial piece of evidence. Honolulu Star-Bulletin *photo*

William K. Clark, sergeant of the police vice squad, was given immunity in return for testimony against fellow policemen. He died in 1948 and Jardine, who had collected the evidence against him, served as one of his pallbearers. *State Archives*

Police Captain Clarence Caminos was the only one of twenty-six indicted policemen to be convicted of bribe-taking in the police graft case. He served thirty-three months in prison and emerged a broken man. *State Archives*

PART 2

19

By-Products of War

THERE were what people call extenuating circumstances for the biggest police scandal Honolulu ever saw, and they all began on the morning of December 7, 1941. When planes of the Japanese navy dropped bombs on Pearl Harbor, the Hawaiian Islands and Honolulu suddenly became one of the most important places on the globe and stayed that way for several years.

Hawaii remained a front bastion of defense as other bastions fell all over the Pacific. These islands were also the springboard for attack, the mustering place for Army, Navy, Marine Corps, and Army Air Force. While local citizens prepared for immediate defense, the military were routing thousands of fighting men and more thousands of tons of fighting equipment through Hawaii. They brought still more thousands of civilian war workers, both male and female, into the islands to do the work that had to be done in shipyards, supply depots, ordnance depots, and offices where reports had to be done at least in triplicate, which made paper work pile ever higher.

The local population waded knee-deep in paper work. A center of this activity was Iolani Palace, the seat of Territorial government, where all kinds of hastily built emergency buildings crowded the place. People bustled about in hurried confusion, the like of which Honolulu has never seen before or since. Say you wanted to buy some chicken feed for a couple of pet bantams. Or floor cleaner. Or iodine. That meant going through channels at the palace because no one knew when Japanese submarines might start knocking off ships bringing supplies from the mainland and chicken feed might have to be eaten by humans. Most of the U.S.

Pacific war fleet, remember, still lay bombed out and burned out at Pearl Harbor.

The first six months after Pearl Harbor was bombed, neither Honolulu nor any of its citizens was anything like normal. Honolulu was the only American city that really saw war first-hand. In these months no one was sure when we might see it again. There were plenty of war nerves in evidence, what with the blackout being enforced by trigger-happy GIs and National Guardsmen, everyone suspecting local Japanese of being everything from spies to saboteurs, or maybe captains of the Japanese navy. There was the big hassle over all sorts of commodities, including whiskey.

This all added up to more police problems than our force ever saw before or since, problems that would have put nearly any police force in a quandary. First of all, the military were top boss and the civilian police had to be a sort of lowly subordinate that provided as much local information as possible and did much of the dirty work, but had comparatively little authority. The military slapped the islands under martial law and kept them that way until all Honolulu was thoroughly sick of it and finally fought its way out through the courts on October 26, 1944.

Then there was the problem of possible traitors, spies, and saboteurs in our midst. Roughly one-third of our population was of Japanese extraction, many of these being second generation, with fairly close ties to Dai Nippon. There were thousands of Japanese aliens in our cities and villages, some of whom never attempted to conceal their allegiance to Hirohito. So what could we expect from them?

What eventually developed, of course, was that two of the finest fighting units in our army, the 100th Infantry Battalion and the 442nd Regimental Combat Team, came from the ranks of what we learned to call Americans of Japanese Ancestry. Many of the aliens were aliens only because they couldn't be naturalized under the laws of that time. Most of them proved as loyal to America as their sons and nephews fighting in Italy. The old-timers who still bowed to pictures of the Son of Heaven in their homes were so far out of touch with the times they couldn't have been a threat to anyone had they chosen to take an active part in the war. And there was no evidence they ever did.

After the intelligence reports were all assimilated and evaluated after the war, the military issued a statement that there had never been any evidence of sabotage or espionage in Hawaii committed by anyone other than official agents of the Japanese government. By the time the report came out, of course, we in Hawaii knew it was the truth. But during the war, especially in the early part, there was a lot of jumpiness among some of our citizens, mostly among the officials and workers, military or otherwise, who had never seen an Oriental before coming to Hawaii.

It wasn't any of these things that caused the big police scandal, though they certainly contributed to the tension of the times. What got our police force into trouble was the fabulous amount of loose money that was suddenly floating all over town. Everyone who could work was working, and that was unusual enough in our easy-going islands. Far more important than that, thousands of soldiers and sailors, who hit Honolulu briefly on their way to some forward Pacific island, literally threw their money around in the town seeking a last thrill, or kick of some sort, before they went into battle. Money meant nothing to them, for in the back of their minds was the thought they might never come back. Too many were right. In addition, war workers here were making more money than they'd ever seen before. Garrison and depot troops were also well-heeled and ready spenders.

With shipping restricted for wartime purposes, there was little that could be imported. Nonessential salable items were soon snatched up by eager buyers. In fact, there was far more money to be spent than there were things to buy with the money. This naturally led to illegal activities. Liquor was often very hard to get except through the armed forces. Enterprising locals went into business distilling rotgut and made money hand over fist. Women were also in short supply even though everyone felt it a patriotic duty to do everything possible to entertain the fighting men. There were women who made more money offering "something for the boys" than they did at their regular jobs.

More notorious were prostitutes who operated illegally but under tacit control of the Police Department.* They now were working shifts around the clock, with soldiers and sailors waiting their turns in long queues to be "serviced" in assembly-line fashion, each being allowed a limit of no more than three minutes. Like author William Bradford Huie's Mamie Stover,† the girls made thousands of dollars, and some were even wise enough to retire to the mainland eventually with comparative wealth. With others it was easy-come, easy-go, and their earnings usually went into the upkeep of some "fancy man."

While prostitutes were among the more obvious of the money-makers, there were others in illegal fields not under the same kind of protected control—or at least not officially so—who had cash in amounts they had never before considered possible. These were the gamblers who profited hugely from the inability of many people to find enough to do with their time. Our gamblers should not be confused with those on the mainland who operate semipublic houses open to all comers. Our gambling houses were never open to servicemen. They were strictly by, of, and for the local boys. The play, however, was heavier during the war than ever before or since for a couple of reasons.

First, with servicemen jamming theaters, dance halls, bars, movies, and all other places of entertainment, there wasn't much left for local people to do. And there were many who would just as soon stay as far away from servicemen as possible. Second, plenty of our local boys were wealthy beyond all previous expectations because servicemen casually tipped taxi drivers and bartenders ten

---

*The term applied to this relationship of the community toward illegal prostitution was "toleration." In September 1941 former Territorial Delegate to Congress Victor S. K. Houston, then a new police commissioner, reported that at least nineteen houses of prostitution in Honolulu and an unnamed number in Wahiawa "appear to be tolerated with the knowledge of the city administration and the police commission in violation of the laws of the Territory. He cited Sections 5710 and 6310 of the Revised Laws of Hawaii which included prostitution among common nuisance and vagrancy offences, and Sections 3247 and 3248 which had to do with enforcement of anti-prostitution measures." Under the system of toleration, police controlled prostitution as a public service to contain a necessary evil since males, including plantation workers, outnumbered females by 45,000. *Honolulu Star-Bulletin,* September 26, 1941.

†*Mamie Stover* is a novel; the character is fictitious.

and twenty dollars, and payed news vendors one dollar for newspapers, and shoeshine boys five dollars for shines they didn't need. That money burned in the pockets of the local boys almost as much as it had when it was in the pockets of the soldiers and sailors.

For these island residents, Chinese gambling houses provided a form of recreation where they could fraternize without interruption from servicemen, who might throw nasty cracks about draft dodgers and get some action for their money at the same time. The money at these games daily ran into thousands, accumulating into millions.

The gamblers, unlike the prostitutes, did not operate by the unwritten but firm sanction of officialdom.* Proprietors of these houses used certain precautions. They employed bouncers to make sure those who entered were local boys, to give the alarm if police raided, and to relieve customers of their weapons, checking them just as hatcheck girls check the headpieces of patrons at night clubs. One proprietor kept six to a dozen vicious dogs in his backyard to discourage police curiosity.

These places were supposed to be subject to arrest at all times. Yet half a dozen or more establishments ran full blast every day. There was an occasional raid but seldom was enough evidence collected to get a conviction. Raiding policemen usually found a number of men sitting around eating or reading magazines as if they were merely assembled at a social club.

There was so much talk that everyone interested in the matter assumed there must be some payoffs somewhere from the gamblers in return for tip-offs about when the raids were coming. But no one could prove it, though I can't remember that anyone had really tried for a long, long time.

*The policy of official toleration of prostitution, described in a previous footnote, ended in 1944 when Honolulu's houses of prostitution were closed in response to a public campaign. Some of the houses then became gambling halls without official sanction.

20

The Punch Felt Round Hawaii

SMACK!

The slender Chinese reeled back from the blow and put his hands to his face. The cop, wearing dungarees and faded aloha shirt, stood with fist clenched ready to hit him again. Several other Chinese watched, emotionless, already in custody of policemen who stood by, clad in the same kind of plain clothes as the officer who had struck the blow.

The small Chinese recovered in a moment and lunged back at the cop. There was nothing chicken about him. He was ready to fight despite his disadvantage in weight and official status, an attitude that gave him some respect on the street. But not with the cop who cocked his fist again.

At that moment, a ranking officer of the Vice Squad pushed his subordinate back. He pushed the Chinese much harder and said to him in words of bitter scorn, "You're through in Chinatown! You're finished!" The slender Chinese showed none of the stoicism often attributed to his people. His black eyes burned with anger as he answered in the best American movie gangster tradition.

"Oh yeah? Well, if I'm through in Chinatown, so is everybody else."

There were more words in this vein. The officer repeated his threat, "So far as I'm concerned, you're through." That meant something. The little Chinese was no gangster, but he was one of a horde of gamblers who had been operating almost openly during the war years. When a ranking member of the Vice Squad said a gambler was through, it carried weight. The Chinese was not the largest nor the most influential gambler operating, so the cops who heard his answer didn't attach much importance to his words. It might have been smarter to do so.

When the feisty little gambler said everybody else was finished if he was, he meant it. First, he filed a complaint of assault against the cop who had struck him. Then he withdrew the complaint and sent word to the captain of the Vice Squad that unless the cop came to apologize within three days, he would blow the top off the gambling setup and expose the police part in it. Still the officers took no heed.

On the fourth day, the gambler sent an emissary to get me and Val Cederlof. We shall call the emissary Ah Sook, which is a kind of John Doe name among Chinese. At any rate, at about 5:30 on the afternoon of March 8, 1946, Val and I went to Ah Sook's house. Two gamblers were waiting for us. One of them was the angry Chinese, Sau Hong Lee, known as Little Snake, and the other we shall call Jimmy the Barber for convenience.

Val and I had never met either of the gamblers before, though we knew who they were by reputation. We realized when Little Snake started talking that what he said could blow the lid off the Police Department. At the same time, we had to consider the source. There are many reasons why a petty criminal will turn stool pigeon. In the first place, a gambler like Little Snake had very little consciousness of being a criminal at all. He had rationalized his crimes to where he saw nothing morally wrong with gambling.

This kind of rationalizing gets a criminal's mind so twisted up that he is quick to condemn the policeman who betrays his trust by taking a bribe, even though the criminal is the one paying the bribe. So he feels superior to the policeman rather than an accomplice in crime. It takes only a comparatively small irritation to turn a criminal like that into a stool pigeon. We knew that Little Snake had turned informer because he got a punch in the jaw from a cop raiding his game.

Both Val and I had this in mind when Little Snake began to tell his story, first about himself and his own gambling history. He said it was this same officer of the Vice Squad who had been responsible back in 1941 for his opening a gambling game in Chinatown.

At that time, said Little Snake, the officer had approached him after he had been arrested in a gambling raid at Ewa, a sugar plantation town. The officer told him he could operate without police interference for $75 a week.

For the first seventeen weeks, Little Snake said, he operated a *pai kau* game on Maunakea Street in the heart of Honolulu's Chinatown while paying $75 a week to the Vice Squad officer. During that time there had been comparatively few "extras." The payoffs had been in various places, most often at the Vice Squadsman's house and on Ala Moana Road near Kewalo Inn.

Little Snake said the first request for an extra came one day when the police officer wanted some venetian blinds and told Little Snake to pay for them. A few days later, the gambler got a call from a furniture store asking if he would pay for the blinds. Little Snake agreed. He said the bill came to something over $140. Another demand for an extra came a few weeks later, according to Little Snake, when the police officer asked for a 16-millimeter movie camera. He said he purchased a camera, projector, and some film for about $190 and had them delivered to the Vice Squadsman's house.

The gambler said his game made money despite the drain of protection money. It was discontinued because of disagreement among Snake's associates rather than financial failure. A couple of years later, after backing other gamblers' games, Snake went into business with some other partners including Jimmy the Barber.

Little Snake said the price of protection had risen greatly by this time along with wartime inflation. When the game started, a Sergeant Bill Clark told the gamblers it would cost $900 a week to stay in operation, Little Snake said, and they paid it for the first eight months. Then, in 1944, they moved from house to house, like the floating crap games of Damon Runyon's New York gamblers, to avoid the sergeant, Snake said. The tactic was not successful.

He said the payoff dropped to $750 a week, then went up again to $900, later to $970. Little Snake said he took a trip to Maui about this time but arranged to have the payoffs to the sergeant continue. When he came back from Maui, he ran a game on Kamanuwai Lane where he ran into another acquaintance from the

Vice Squad who wanted money as usual, but was no longer in a position to be very demanding since he was off the squad. Little Snake said he gave him only $25 and the officer got angry.

By early 1945, the sergeant's demand had come down to $500, Little Snake said, because there were so many such sources of income that the sergeant could offer bargain rates to old customers. Little Snake insisted this cop was so brazen he would park his car on Maunakea Street in the middle of Chinatown every Tuesday and wait for the payoffs to come in.

Before long, Sergeant Clark had an extra request, a blue feather lei, Little Snake said. A feather lei is a hatband made of pheasant feathers and worn with much pride by old-time Hawaiians and *kamaaina* residents of the islands. The sergeant wanted his lei an inch wider than the regular size, according to Snake. He said he agreed to get one on his next trip to Maui and that he paid $75 for the lei, specially made. We all agreed that it was a bargain.

It was very late that night when Val and I went home full of Chinese food and with a stimulating amount of good liquor under our belts. We had leads on the biggest Chinese gamblers in town, some bigger than Little Snake, leads that might close down the gamblers, something the Vice Squad had not been able to do. Also for the first time, we had leads on payoffs to the Vice Squad.

I can't say I was happy about that part. The men Little Snake claimed to have paid off were brother police officers. I had worked with some of them. I counted Sergeant Clark a long-time friend. Better than most people, I knew the temptation they felt as cops with modest incomes suddenly given a chance to make easy money. They must have told themselves they weren't hurting anyone by squeezing the gamblers a little. I felt sorry for them.

Yet another part of me as a cop was disgusted and angry. Any cop who takes a bribe is betraying a trust he is paid to protect. He is just like any other crook, only a little less honest. A burglar or stickup artist takes his chances outside the law. When a cop on the Police Force turns into a crook, it's the same as stealing from his own family. As much as I hated to, it was my duty to investigate these leads about bribes.

Next, Val and I approached the gambler I've called Jimmy the

Barber. His story was substantially the same as Snake's. He said the sergeant had approached him in August 1943 to ask when he was going to open up a game. The Barber said he remonstrated that he had no chance, with police pinching gamblers, but that the sergeant had disagreed.

According to the Barber, the sergeant had told him, "You just have to pay the overhead. It comes to $900 a week. That's what everybody pays me."

The Barber said he formed a combination and set up a fan-tan game under protection, which the sergeant raided once in awhile anyhow, possibly to show his superiors he was cracking down or to emphasize the need for continued payoffs. The Barber said he didn't know which. After paying the sergeant a total of $7,200 over the weeks, he said he got disgusted and let another partner in the game to do the paying, although he retained a share up until the time he was speaking to us. The Barber consulted his expense book and told us the payoffs had risen from $900 a week to $1,070 in the meantime.

A day or so later, we talked to a gambler we'll call Mussolini and got still another story of payoffs. Mussolini said a Vice Squad captain had offered, through a go-between, to let him run his game for $1,400 a week. The gambler objected that the price was too high and offered $850. He said the captain wouldn't agree to any such discount and the deal fell flat. Mussolini maintained that the cop who had acted as go-between wanted $200 for his trouble in the dickering but was persuaded to accept $25, though with bad grace.

It seemed time to tell the story to our boss, Prosecutor William Z. Fairbanks. We did. The prosecutor immediately wanted to hear the stories himself and have them taken down. We made a date with all the gamblers we had talked to thus far to meet the prosecutor at Val Cederlof's house, with a stenographer present.

The first thing the Chinese wanted to know was, "What about immunity?" After all, if the police were guilty of taking bribes, so were the gamblers guilty of paying them. Bill Fairbanks told them he couldn't promise immunity. If they wanted to testify and take their chances, the government would recognize that they had cooperated and their action would be considered heavily in their favor. That was all.

The four gamblers then politely told us they wanted to confer on the matter. They withdrew to the other side of the room. There was no need to go farther, for they all spoke Cantonese and were reasonably sure none of us did. They were right. (I have pondered over how much help a good working knowledge of Cantonese or Japanese or Filipino dialects would be to a non-Oriental detective in Honolulu.) The gamblers made up their minds pretty quickly. They turned back to us and said they had agreed to talk even if they went to prison for it. Through the next several hours, they gave their statements while our stenographer took everything down. The stories were the same ones they had told Val and me earlier.

Back in the office the next day, we considered how to make the best use of what we had. Obviously, there was a lot more questioning to be done. But first we contacted a tax examiner in the U.S. Bureau of Field Examiners, a friend of ours, and tipped him off that something big was afoot. I suggested that he make a cautious check of local banks and trust companies to find out whether any of the police officers whose names I gave him had commercial or savings accounts, or safe-deposit boxes, and to let me know. A week later the field examiner called back to say that he had found a box rented in the name of Sergeant Clark on July 14, 1944, at one of Honolulu's large banks. He had also located a smaller account at a branch bank at Schofield Barracks in the name of a police captain.

Val Cederlof and I took this information to John Glutsch, special agent in charge of the intelligence unit of the Bureau of Internal Revenue. We told him we would keep him informed of the progress of the investigation and give him a report when we were finished. He agreed to cooperate with us.

Getting the truth from gamblers was much more difficult. By now Chinatown was buzzing. When we approached one of the gamblers, we could tell he already knew what the score was. Many were not willing to tell us what they knew. They were suspicious of all cops, including us. They were even suspicious of each other.

185

One chunky, bespectacled man who spoke little English merely told us over and over again, "Me no like talk." But there were some who confirmed Little Snake's story and those of his three friends.

Still, all we had was the stories of gamblers. Very carefully, we chose a police officer or two who might be able to corroborate some of the evidence. We had to be careful to ask questions without tipping our hand as to the scope of the whole thing. One policeman remembered riding in the car with Sergeant Clark that day he received a blue feather lei. The same man recalled it was supposed to have come from Maui.

Bill Fairbanks realized, of course, that he was getting into something pretty big and so touchy he would have to handle it with wisdom. Who could say how high the graft went? Who could be trusted? By this time, when we added the payoffs reported by the other gamblers we had questioned, the sergeant's total take in alleged bribes came to $116,280. Finally, Fairbanks told one police commissioner the whole story. The commissioner was shocked, especially when he learned the size of the take we had uncovered. Fairbanks asked the commissioner not to tell anyone, not even other members of the commission. This he agreed to do.

But Little Snake refused to wait for our move. He told a former Vice Squad captain what was happening. The captain went to see the chairman of the Police Commission, Warren G. McDermid. The chairman called Little Snake in and heard the story for himself. Then he went to Attorney General Nils Tavares. The story finally reached the acting governor, who allocated $15,000 for an investigation of police graft.

Several weeks had gone by. As yet, virtually none of this was known to the general public, though wild rumors were spreading in the Police Department. Some decisions had to be made. It was decided by those in charge that the investigation would be handled jointly by the attorney general, the police commission, and the Honolulu public prosecutor who was by Territorial law a deputy of the attorney general. But who would do the investigating?

I had made my feelings on the subject pretty clear to Val Cederlof. I wanted no part of the investigation. After being a cop for more than twenty years, I had no desire to be the one to dig up dirt on my brother officers, even though I was positive by now such dirt existed. A thorough investigation would have to be made of those named by the gamblers. Criminal prosecutions might follow. I knew I would be regarded with hostility by the officers I would have to investigate. I regarded the sergeant as a friend. We had worked on a number of cases together.

A few days later, Fairbanks called Val into his office and told him he would be assigned to the investigation. My partner asked if I were going to work on the case, too.

"Of course," Fairbanks answered.

"I don't think so," Val answered.

Fairbanks was surprised and asked, "Why not?"

So Val told him about my feelings. Fairbanks immediately sent Val out to tell me to come into his office. I explained to the prosecutor why I didn't think I should be assigned to the case. I told him I was a cop, after all, and I didn't think it would be suitable for me to investigate other policemen. Fairbanks listened patiently. When I was finished he asked a question:

"Is there anything crooked about you?"

"No, nothing."

"Is there anything bothering your conscience?"

"No, no. There's nothing like that."

He paused as he considered my request before he answered, "Then I want you to work with Val on the case."*

There was nothing much left for me to say. Things started happening pretty quickly after that. Within the week, Attorney General Tavares and Prosecutor Fairbanks held a conference in the former's office at Iolani Palace and decided to call the police commission in the next day and inform the members of our findings.

It began at nine o'clock in the morning with the police commissioners filtering in one at a time to Attorney General Tavares' office at Iolani Palace, at different times and by different entrances

---

*William Z. Fairbanks, who became a circuit judge, said later he considered Cederlof and Jardine an excellent team of investigators. He said they complemented each other, Cederlof being the quicker of the two, Jardine the most determined. He said both had his absolute trust and that they sometimes disagreed with him.

to avoid tipping the newspapers. Reporters who covered the palace* had sniffed out something was afoot with the police, but they didn't know much. We didn't want them to until we could question the policemen involved.

When the commissioners were assembled, Tavares and Fairbanks quickly outlined the stories we had taken from the Chinese gamblers, and Val read excerpts from some of the statements. The commissioners responded strongly and said they expected the law against gambling to be enforced to the limit. They favored taking any steps necessary to prosecute any police officers who had taken protection money from gamblers. They agreed to back the investigation all the way and that it should be conducted jointly by the attorney general and public prosecutor and the police commission.

The next move that morning was to call in Police Chief W. A. Gabrielson and tell him that some of his officers were to be questioned on graft charges. He took the news calmly, saying he had always warned his men against taking bribes. Gabrielson promised his cooperation. Then, at the request of the attorney general, the chairman of the commission ordered the chief to have the officers picked up for questioning about the statements of the gamblers.

All of that was done in less than an hour. By shortly after ten o'clock, Val and I were back at our office in City Hall. Val took Louis Comacho, a police detective assigned to the prosecutor's office, down and staked him out at the sergeant's safe-deposit box. Antone Manuel, one of the attorney general's investigators, was assigned to the bank with orders to arrest anyone, including the sergeant, should they attempt to open the box.

Then we were back at our office again, ready to question the accused officers who had been brought to City Hall. Three of them had been called from duty, but the sergeant had been on leave and had been picked up at home. Chief Gabrielson had been ordered to assign patrolmen to guard the interrogation room to make sure no reporters or other unauthorized persons got too close. What with the attorney general, the public prosecutor, most of the police commission, the chief himself, and the accused officers having dis-

*Iolani Palace was the seat of the Territorial government at the time, housing offices of the governor and his cabinet. The Territorial legislature also met there.

appeared into our office, excitement buzzed through the whole building.

Inside the office, the interrogation began with me asking most of the questions, Chief Gabrielson and the commissioners sitting as an audience. A police lieutenant came first. He denied everything, stating that he had never taken anything from any gamblers either in money or extras. Next came Sergeant Clark. He denied all charges of receiving anything from gamblers. On questioning, he said there was nothing in his safe-deposit box but $3,500 worth of war bonds and about $500 in cash. He refused to give anyone permission to go through the box, which was his right.

When asked if he'd ordered and received a blue pheasant lei from Little Snake, he answered, "What would I want with a pheasant lei? I never wear a hat."

The next policeman, Captain Caminos, appeared cooperative. He told us we could go through his safe-deposit box. Later in the day, men of the Territorial tax office rode with him to Schofield. When they opened the box, there was nothing in it to incriminate the captain. He told us that he owned, besides his home in Wahiawa, a beach home at Mokuleia, three lots in Wahiawa, and a home near the volcano of Kilauea on the island of Hawaii. But that didn't prove anything.

So it went, day after day. Another police captain named by the gamblers as having been in on the payoffs denied he had received money from any gamblers or had ever negotiated for any. The parade of witnesses continued all week, from both Chinatown and the Police Department. We called the accused officers back again and again, with no results. By this time newspapers were getting the story, though not from us, and it made daily headlines. The police officers we questioned made no public statements. In the interrogation room we got no admissions of guilt, only statements of innocence.

There was one new development at this time. I had come home about 1 A.M. after a long night session and had gone to bed after my usual late snack. It seemed to me I had just gone to sleep when the telephone rang. I lifted the receiver and heard a voice before I said a word.

"John, is that you?"

I recognized the voice of my old friend we have called Ah Sook.

"Call a taxi and come over right away," he said. "I'll pay the fare."

I glanced at the clock and saw it was 4 A.M.

"Look, can't it wait till later in the morning?" I said. "I just went to sleep a little while ago."

"No, no, you come now. It's important."

In twenty minutes I was in Ah Sook's part of town. I dismissed the taxi and walked a block to his house, where a light was burning. The Chinese smiled politely as he opened the door and waved me inside. Then he poured half a glass of fine Bourbon and asked about my health. I knew he hadn't called me at four o'clock in the morning to offer me a drink. Just the same, I took it and, after pouring it down, I began to wake up.

"How's the investigation coming?" he asked.

"Fine," I answered, waiting for the verbal sparring to be over so Ah Sook could come to the point.

"Gee, it don't look so good, eh?"

"Yeah. It looks bad for some grafting cops and maybe some tax evaders."

Ah Sook's face lost the polite smile and became very serious.

"That's what I want to talk to you about. If this thing all comes out, a lot of my friends are going to be stuck with taxes. It looks like some of them just thought of it."

Then Ah Sook brought out what was really in his mind. Somewhat belatedly, the gamblers had figured out that Uncle Sam was going to be interested in all the evidence of big money being thrown around. Sooner or later, somebody would be asking where the gamblers got the money they said they'd been paying off the cops with and why they hadn't filed income tax reports on it. Likewise, T-men would be digging to find out how much more hadn't been reported, and before they were through, somebody would be in big trouble.

Gradually Ah Sook got around to making his proposition. He wanted Val and me to kill the investigation and he had an idea how we could do it. To outward appearances, we would work as hard as ever. We would do a lot of paper shuffling and wind up with a hefty report that had nothing inside to cause any charges against anybody. Ah Sook ended his little speech with: "You can make yourself forty or fifty thousand dollars."

I smiled and poured another drink, trying to move slow and think fast. The price was higher than I figured because you don't talk about amounts of money like that unless you're ready to hand over a lot more. You might offer forty thousand. Or you might offer fifty thousand. But you don't offer one or the other if you mean it. Nobody in his right mind would take the lesser amount.

"How about Val?" I asked. "He's a good friend of yours."

It was Val who had introduced Ah Sook to me. Val knew him much better than I did.

"Never mind about Val," said Ah Sook. "He and his wife are pretty well fixed. But you're not. I looked you up."

"Is that why you came to me?"

"Sure. But there's another reason. You've known Val for years. You've worked with him. The two of you are partners, close friends. You can talk to him a lot better than I can."

It might sound better if I said I rejected the offer immediately and stalked out of the place. But it wouldn't be true. I led Ah Sook on a little more. Looking back on it, I guess I was leading myself on, too. Fifty thousand dollars is a lot of money to a cop who, after twenty years on the force, had no house, no lot, no land, not even a car.

"You know I never took a nickel in my life," I told Ah Sook. "Now I'll tell you the truth. If I'm going to take something this time, it's got to be big, a lot bigger than the money you're talking about."

The Chinese wasn't a bit surprised. "How big?" he shot back.

We started kicking it around, with me stressing all the risks there would be in trying to kill the investigation by producing nothing but a mass of unimportant evidence. Actually, in my own mind I knew there wouldn't be anything very hard about it. The only danger might be that our bosses would get impatient and assign some different investigators to replace us. But by that time, Val and I would have collected our money.

191

I knew there wasn't much to fear from Ah Sook, that he'd spill to the law and expose us. Ah Sook had once been arrested in an opium smuggling racket. He had gone through a trial to conviction and had done time in a federal prison without ever naming any accomplices, though it was common knowledge he had them. Also, he had now run up a fortune of half a million dollars. His word was good for whatever amount he said.

Finally, we agreed that a figure of $75,000 might be fair. I would do the talking to Val and I would receive the money in cash from Ah Sook and split half-and-half with Val. It was all settled except for one thing. All along, I knew I couldn't sell my soul. So I quit stalling and daydreaming and told Ah Sook so. He wasn't surprised about that, either. In fact, he reacted as if he'd been expecting me to refuse. Ah Sook had seen a lot of life. He was a very hard man to surprise.

"All right," he said. "But don't tell anyone, not even Val."

Then I realized he had been worried for fear I'd run him in for trying to bribe a policeman. I couldn't have, of course. But there was an even better reason not to. A police detective is only as good as his sources. Ah Sook was one of the best. That ended a pleasant half hour of playing with temptation.

I walked out without any money. Yet I had a fine family, good children, and a pretty good reputation. I was counting them high that morning when I came out of Ah Sook's house into the gray dawn. I was feeling pretty good in spite of my lack of sleep. It isn't every morning you have a chance to turn down a fortune and prove you're honest. I could even have run up the bidding a lot higher.

21

Gabrielson Goes Out

THINGS began happening late in March 1946. Two members of the Vice Squad were suspended for thirty days by Chief Gabrielson and the police commission announced a complete reorganization of the squad. But no charges had been filed against anybody. It was a frustrating time for Val and me, and we knew it would get a lot more frustrating before we were finished.

Some of the cops on the force had become very unfriendly toward us. Maybe they had a right to be. At a time like that, we didn't know who to trust. One of the most dangerous men in town, a graduate of San Quentin who happened to be friendly with Val, came and told us he had heard that some of the accused cops were planning to shoot us in the back. He suggested that he tail along behind at a distance and protect us. We rejected the offer. How did we know whether he was motivated by friendship for us or by dislike for one of the cops he wanted to get a shot at?

The one man who didn't carry a grudge was Sergeant Bill Clark. He was a big, amiable Hawaiian who had been a great football player twenty years before. He was known as a good fellow by almost everyone in town. Going over the list, Val and I figured him for the key man. But we couldn't get anything important out of him, even though it was just as easy to talk to him after the beginning of the investigation as before. He hardly bothered to deny his guilt. But he wouldn't make any statements. Our visits with him were more like informal chats between old-timers on the force. I remember my last visit to his house, along with Val, when he invited us into his bedroom where we sat and chewed the fat.

"I hate to keep bringing this up about the graft," I said finally. "But you know that's our job. That's what we're supposed to be working on. What I want to ask now is, if you should change your mind and decide to make a statement, or open your safe-deposit box, or anything like that, how about letting Val and me know?"

"Sure, sure," he nodded. "If I decide to do it, I'll give you guys the first break."

When we left, he loaded me down with a bag of mangoes and gave Val a couple.

"I'm giving John more because he has kids," he told Val.

At least, Chief Gabrielson was on the skids. The responsibility for the scandal was his. Val and I knew that the police commissioners felt he had not done very much about investigating corruption on his own even after it had been brought to his attention. We learned from a cabinet official at Iolani Palace that word had gone down from the governor's office to fire Gabrielson. Fairbanks was to pass the word to the police commission.

But on April 1, the date set for firing, a tidal wave hit the islands, especially the Hilo waterfront. It was one of the biggest disasters in our history; 201 lives were lost and property damage ran into millions. So the firing was held up. By April 12, Val and I were getting impatient to see some results. We went in to light a fire under the boss. He was a good guy but he didn't appreciate us telling him what to do. Fairbanks said he'd act when he was good and ready. By that time, Val and I were steamed up. We said, "To hell with you," or words to that effect, and stormed out of the office.*

We marched out of the building and got into Val's car to drive to a bar on the edge of Waikiki to have a few drinks and cool off. It was about nine o'clock. We sat there feeling sorry for ourselves, suspicious of everybody. At eleven o'clock the radio in the bar car-

---

*Fairbanks said later that Jardine was an individualist with a temper. He was also independent. "He was a good man to have working for you," said Fairbanks. "He was a man who questioned your judgment at times. Jardine knew his business. When you have a man like that, you leave him alone. I treated men not as if they were working for me, but as if they were working with me."

ried the news that Chief Gabrielson had resigned.* Bill Fairbanks had worked fast. That affected us more than the drinks. Now what? Would he take our resignations too? Not many special investigators are stupid enough to tell off the boss and spend the rest of the day getting tanked up.

Fairbanks didn't leave us in doubt long. That night a circuit court judge came around to visit Val at his home to let us know that all was forgiven—if there was anything to forgive. As big-hearted a man as he was an able prosecutor, Fairbanks ignored the whole episode as if it had never happened. Besides, the investigation had just started and he needed us more than ever.

What made it hard was Captain Caminos, a police captain the gamblers liked, even though he was milking them. We got evidence that this cop started on the take long before World War II, in Wahiawa, a rural town not far from Schofield Barracks. Wahiawa is surrounded by pineapple fields. Many of the workers are Filipino, often single men who left their families behind in the Philippines. For a lot of the older men, the chief recreation on weekends at the time was gambling on cards, dice, and cockfights. With them, cockfighting was a national sport at home and one they had not given up in Hawaii, though it was against the law.

This police captain took money from every cockfight promoter who would pay him. One Filipino proprietor of dice games and cockfights told us, "He give me chance to run three weeks. Number four week, he catch me, catch chicken. He catch me one time every month." The gambler said he levied a "protection tax" of $1 for every two passes of the dice to make up the $25 weekly fee for the captain. At Christmas and New Year's, the price doubled.

Another Filipino gambler ran a small dice game in his home close to the Waialua fire station. He told us how he got raided in 1944 and forfeited bail along with his players. When the court

*A police commission statement made at the time of Gabrielson's resignation said he was leaving because his wife needed an operation on the mainland and that his resignation had nothing to do with the graft investigation. Later news stories (*Honolulu Star-Bulletin,* March 27, 1947 and November 1, 1978) said he was to be fired for failure to clean up the department, but was granted the privilege of resigning.

action was finished, the captain came to him and told him he could run the game and make back the money he had forfeited in court if he would pay $20 a week for protection.

The gambler agreed and ran for more than two months when the captain decided he wanted an extra, the nice outboard motor-boat his gambler client possessed. The gambler stalled because the boat had cost him $550 and he wasn't rolling in money the way the Chinatown gamblers were. But the captain kept after him until the Filipino gave in. A few days later, the captain came with a truck and a Hawaiian helper and took the boat away. It wasn't until the war came along that the captain became head of the Vice Squad in Honolulu, where he could make big money.

But, as I said, everybody liked Captain Caminos. After telling us all this, the gambler added that he'd given up the boat because he was grateful to the captain for letting him run his game as long as he did. I learned later that Little Snake had tipped off the captain before blowing the lid off police graft. He had had plenty of time to clear out his safe-deposit box.

Another problem was the kind of witnesses we had to depend on. They were all gamblers with bones to pick and fish to fry. The biggest operator of them all was Paul S. F. Au. He said he was willing to talk because he didn't get the protection he paid for. Night after night, the three of us sat on the floor of Val's house while Au sang. Like Little Snake, he firmly believed there was nothing morally wrong with gambling and he was quick to condemn policemen. With a man like that, it's hard to know where the truth begins.

Au had trafficked in women before becoming Honolulu's biggest gambling impresario. His Honolulu Rooms, used as a forty-room house of prostitution before and a dance hall later, then a gambling house, was located half a block from Aala Park in the heart of Honolulu's slums. The location was perfect. Thousands of longshoremen and workers from the navy yard lived within a few blocks. Au could afford to be choosey. He allowed only Chinese and Filipinos and an occasional Japanese to play the fan-tan and dice his house afforded. Once he served fine Chinese food free of charge to players who happened to be there at the time.

For protection he had a licensed private detective and a 250-pound wrestler at the front door searching the persons seeking entry, taking their guns, knives, and other weapons the way a hat-check girl checks hats. Inside, two Filipinos strode here and there among the tables, cane knives strapped to their belts, to keep order among the players. In the yard behind, half a dozen vicious police dogs kept a noisy watch against intruders like the police.

Au told Val and me he was sick and tired of those crooks, grafters, and double-crossers on the police force. He said he wanted to free his conscience and that he didn't want to carry the thought of his relationship with these crooks on his mind. In other words, he made himself out as the injured party. He also pled poverty. He claimed to have in cash only $6,500 in the Bank of Hawaii and another $2,000 in the Bishop National Bank.* In property, he said he owned the Honolulu Rooms with his wife but that it was mortgaged to the Bank of Hawaii, the balance being $50,000. He also owned four old houses on Liliha Street, a semislum section of town, two pieces of property that he was leasing, and his wife had a house on Liliha Street which was at the time vacant.

If what he said was straight, the wages of sin were surprisingly low. But I never took that statement at face value. He told us his payoff total was $144,035. That had to be only a fraction of his income as a gambling house proprietor. I remember too well the years when he had forty prostitutes paying $75 a day for units in the Honolulu Rooms. That comes to a little more than a million dollars a year. I'm willing to bet that Paul Au made a lot more money than he reported.

As for his payoffs as a gambler, that began when Governor Ingram M. Stainback ordered houses of prostitution closed on September 20, 1944, and Au was put out of business along with prostitutes and other proprietors. He said that some time in January 1945 he gave the patrol officer on the beat in which Honolulu Rooms was located $50 because the officer had first suggested the system of searching gamblers for weapons before they entered to play.

*Bishop National Bank is now First Hawaiian Bank.

197

Later, he said, he began making protection payments to the captain of the Vice Squad and to the sergeant who told him he was "taking care of the boys" out of his payment. Au named sums of $1,000 a week for the captain and $900 for the sergeant. That $1,000 got reduced to $500 and then $300 a week, Au said, because he was buying a lot of food and other luxuries for the captain. He named eggs, roasts and steaks, slabs of ham and bacon, butter, squid, pork, and various Chinese foods, most of which he got on the black market. In addition, Au said, there was whiskey and cigarets, which the captain hauled away in an old patrol wagon.

Au said that in March of 1945 the sergeant tipped him off about a visit from a Filipino officer in plain clothes assigned by Chief Gabrielson to gain admittance to the Honolulu Rooms. By the time the undercover man got there, the game was closed down. By July, Au's payoffs had risen to $3,700 per week, he said, plus whatever he spent for black market food and cigars.

The gambler gave us another story about a tip-off on a gambling raid led by Chief Gabrielson himself. About noon of January 19, 1946, he said, he got a call from the sergeant telling him to "watch good today." Looking back on it, Au said it was the kind of crack the sergeant could claim was intended as a tip-off yet in itself didn't mean much. Au said he let the games run. But about 2 P.M. a girl working for him got a call from the captain telling her to tell Au to close the place up, that the cops would raid in about twenty minutes. According to the story from Au, his girl gave him the message and he called the captain, who verified it, saying a search warrant would be used.

At this, the gambler said he stopped the games and had all the gambling paraphernalia put away. The customers sat around at the tables playing checkers and reading magazines. An hour went by and the gamblers began to get restless, Au said, arguing that maybe it was a false alarm after all and wanting to start the games again.

When the police did arrive, Au said, it was obvious at once that this raid was something special. Chief Gabrielson led the raiders, accompanied by the captain of vice and the sergeant, both trying

198

to look as though this was what they'd rather do most of all, Au told us. The captain served Au with the warrant and told him to put it in his pocket. Au said he followed the captain to the back of the room where the captain told him, "This is the chief's raid. I don't want my share now."

It was a big raid even though it didn't catch anybody gambling. In all, 173 persons, including Au, were taken to the station and booked. Au seemed proud of the fact that so many of the gamblers had enough faith in him to stay around even after they had word of a raid. He said a lot of them had left by the time the police got there, of course.

Au was a personable gambler who had thought out a lot of angles about the consequences of his giving evidence against the cops, including the danger he'd run of going to jail on income tax violations. He made a clear statement that he had defrauded both the federal and Territorial government in the matter of taxes.

Val and I both knew that a witness like Au would not come to court with clean hands and he might have mixed motives for the stories he told on the cops. But we were assigned to investigate police graft. Our biggest problem was that you seldom find ministers of the gospel, school teachers, bankers, or other respected citizens in the community to appear as witnesses in a police graft case. You take what you can get, and though they are witnesses with checkered backgrounds, you do your best to make the jury believe your evidence.

22

The Greedy Tax Collector

Up to this time, no action had been taken in the police graft case except the suspension of four policemen and the filing of Chief Gabrielson's resignation. He was replaced by a veteran on the force, William Hoopai, who had been assistant chief. Gabrielson took a job in Japan as police administrator in the headquarters of General Douglas MacArthur.

On Saturday, April 27, 1946, *The Advertiser* ran an editorial asking, "Has The Police Scandal Collapsed? What has become of the soul searching, fact finding, revelation-roaring police department investigation? Whipped into a fury of anticipation by tales of lie detectors in use, suspension of officials, great things to come, the public is beginning to wonder if they are being lulled into a state of coma by the old technique of 'play it out and they'll forget it.' "

The investigation was continuing, all right, but we couldn't try our case in the newspapers. Our list of suspects kept growing longer and longer. Then, as so often happens when you start out to catch a criminal, you wind up catching somebody you hadn't even known about beforehand. It all began while we were interrogating Paul Au. He told us that late in January 1946 he got a telephone call from a man named Koon Wah Lee who invited him to call at his home that night if he wished to hear news of much interest. A man with as many fish to fry as Paul Au couldn't refuse an invitation like that even if he wished to. He was there at the appointed time.

Lee, it turned out, was deputy collector in the local office of the U.S. Bureau of Internal Revenue. Lately he had been down at the police station where he had heard Chief Gabrielson say that, while they might not be able to catch Au on a gambling rap, the chief thought he could probably be had on income tax evasion.

Income tax evasion was a subject much in the minds of the gamblers just then. But Au told us that Lee pointed out to him even more dangers ahead. Had Au paid social security taxes for his employees? The gambler, while doing business under cover, employed a big Samoan who watched the door and checked the players' knives and blackjacks, also a former private detective who acted as watchman and fed the big dogs in the back yard, and various women who worked around the place. Then there were the house men who helped run the game. Au had not paid the required taxes.

In the conversation described by Au, Lee told him that was too bad, but it wasn't beyond hope—not if he had a friend in the internal revenue office. The whole matter could be cleared up in return for some money to pay the right people. Au said he'd think about it and left. For nearly a week nothing happened.

Then, Au said, Lee stopped by the Honolulu Rooms and told him it would cost $7,000 to have everything fixed up. The gambler said he agreed, and Lee set to work fixing up the records of some of the employees. But he didn't finish the job. Instead, according to Au, he said he needed $7,000, in addition to back tax payments, to pay off a couple of the boys down at the office. Au did not demur. He said he gave Lee a check for $1,271.50 to cover the tax discrepancies of his employees and promised to have the $7,000 ready later.

Continuing his story, Au said Lee was back on January 30 to fix up some more tax records. Au told him to come back the next day for the $7,000. Then the gambler set the stage for this payoff. The next day he went to the bank and changed $6,000 in small bills to $20 bills, a transaction that was recorded by the bank teller as Au had planned. About noon, he said, Lee telephoned to say he would be right up to get the money. Au said he had two witnesses set and waiting, a man and a woman. He showed them the money wrapped in a newspaper. When Lee arrived, they saw Au hand him the package.

201

No one with experience would have taken a payoff in front of witnesses. But Lee apparently wasn't used to deals of this sort, or his greed outweighed his sense of caution. When Paul Au gave us the details five months later, we had little trouble getting corroborating witnesses. Au had even instructed his employees to count the money and make up the payoff bundle themselves. Nor had he used only his employees as witnesses. Au had called in a contractor working on a carpentry job nearby to watch the transaction.

Late in the evening of May 6, 1946, Val Cederlof and I arrested Lee at his home and brought him down to our office to answer some questions. He came, looking very nervous, and he got more nervous as time went on. We asked him about the money he had received from Au, and he asked to call his lawyer. His attorney advised him to make no statements. But we kept asking questions anyhow and, a time or two, jarred him out of silence.

"Did you receive a newspaper-wrapped package with $7,000 inside?" I repeated.

"I received a package of squid," Lee answered. "This is all a frame-up. I don't know what you're talking about."

"You mean to say we're framing you?"

"Yes, you folks are framing me. You go up and see Paul."

Then I had the stenographer read all the statements of the witnesses from Au's testimony. I asked Lee what he had to say about that. He didn't have a thing to say. When the session ended and Lee went to the lavatory, there was Paul Au in the hallway waiting his turn to be questioned. Lee talked to him in Chinese. Au told us later that Lee had urged him not to admit anything, that he still had the $7,000 and would return it the next day.

Later that evening, at 10:25, Val and I took Lee to the police station lockup and had him booked for investigation. The next morning we questioned him again, but he wouldn't open his mouth. We released him at five o'clock that afternoon pending investigation by John Glutsch, head of the intelligence unit, Bureau of Internal Revenue, and the U.S. district attorney.

Koon Wah Lee was shortly suspended by the Bureau, later indicted, tried, and convicted in federal court. The conviction was later set aside, but he was again indicted by the federal grand jury on a charge of income tax evasion. On June 12, 1947, he entered a plea of nolo contendere. He was fined $2,000 on this charge.

The assistant district attorney then entered an information against him charging that he had accepted for his own use and benefit the $7,000 from Paul Au. Lee pled guilty to the charge and was sentenced to a year and a day in the penitentiary. The execution of this sentence was suspended and he was placed on probation for three years. In addition he was fined $1,500. He never had to go to prison.

23

The Sergeant Confesses

THE period from March 12 to June 22, when Val and I pretty much wrapped up our investigation, seemed to us a whole lifetime. We were tired. We had always worked after regular quitting time, sometimes all night. Totaling it up, we found we had put in 566 hours of overtime, almost 71 days. Add to that the strain of investigating our own brother officers.

There had been little chance for rest or sleep. Things broke too big and too fast for that. There were too many witnesses, both friendly and hostile, who had to be interviewed as soon as possible, before they could hear the rumors and make up alibis. So we were plenty tired and we still didn't have our reports done. That took a long time. Both Val and I were sent alternately to the mainland to bring back prisoners extradited from different states to be tried for crimes in Hawaii. Bill Fairbanks left for San Francisco to argue a case before the Ninth Circuit Court of Appeals. So nothing much happened through the summer.*

Then came the election. A lot of governmental processes slow down around election time. Nobody wants to make the voters angry. When the dust had settled, a whole new city administration had been voted in. We got a new mayor, Johnny Wilson, one of Hawaii's most colorful political figures. He was part-Tahitian, part-Hawaiian, the son of the marshal who had served Queen Liliuokalani in the last days of the Hawaiian Monarchy. The queen herself had sent Johnny to Leland Stanford University where he was a classmate and became a lifelong friend of Herbert Hoover.

It was no great surprise when Mayor Wilson announced that he was appointing as public prosecutor Joseph V. Esposito, an attor-

---

*Public Prosecutor Fairbanks said later he didn't think the police graft cases could be won. He said it came down to whether one believed gamblers or the police, and added, "People would rather believe the police. Usually they are right. By and large, they are honest."

ney almost as colorful as himself. Esposito, of Italian ancestry, came from New England. He had been a doctor and had practiced medicine before taking up law. He was known as a brilliant defense lawyer with a vivid imagination and biting sarcasm that made him a terror on cross-examinations. As a prosecutor he was an unknown quantity. But no one doubted that whatever he did would be interesting.

After the November elections, the town sat back to see what would happen in January after the new mayor and public prosecutor were sworn in. By this time, the police graft investigation had become common knowledge. Val and I had turned in our reports but had made no statements to the press or anybody else. Rumors and charges of corruption had been heard against many policemen. When were they going to be either proved or disproved?

The Advertiser devoted an editorial to the situation:

"When the police inquiry was first undertaken, prior to the resignation of Chief Gabrielson, great promises were made of what would be done in the way of a cleanup. A few cases were brought into the open. Not all of them. The rest were shrouded in a cloud of doubletalk that tapered off to a whisper and finally all but died out."

In past years, Esposito and I had always been on opposite sides of a case, him as defense attorney and me as witness for the prosecution. He had put me over the jumps a number of times and we had exchanged some spirited jabs in court. So as soon as he took office, I went in to congratulate him on the appointment and to ask if he wanted me to remain on the job or to go back to police headquarters.

"Do I have to sign anything to keep you here?" he asked.

"No, your word is sufficient."

"Then it's settled," he said. "You stay here."

Now that Val and I had completed the investigation, the police graft case was out of our hands. What happened from here on was up to the prosecutor. So it was gratifying to see Esposito dig into the mass of reports. He asked us a lot of questions. For instance, who would be a good special prosecutor? We suggested Edward N. Sylva, a former deputy prosecutor. Though Sylva was a Republican and Esposito an active Democrat, he went along with our recommendation. We also told him that in our opinion the sergeant under investigation was the best prospect to spill the works.

Esposito must have been a good listener. Not long after that, toward the end of January, Val and I drove him home at the end of the day. Grinning, he told us the sergeant had made a confession and had told him what was in the safe-deposit box. We couldn't blame the prosecutor for being proud of himself. He had stepped in and gotten a confession where we, the detectives, had failed. But then we didn't have power to offer immunity. Esposito did.

It was the big break in the case. In return for immunity, Sergeant William K. Clark gave Val and me his story in firsthand detail. Clark named the gamblers from whom he had collected, and he named police officers for whom he had been the go-between. He said he had received nearly half a million dollars in bribes, and that the $125,000 he had in his safe-deposit box represented only his share. The rest had been passed on to brother officers for whom he collected. Clark's confession led to a rash of suspensions of officers in the Police Department.*

There were some bizarre turnings in the story of Sergeant Clark, the big, burly police veteran. While he freely admitted taking bribes from gamblers, he insisted, "I never took any money from a prostitute. That's blood money and I don't want any of it. I took from the gamblers because that doesn't hurt anybody." He said he had finally decided to confess after getting advice from two lawyers to turn state's evidence and ask for immunity.

There was another side to his confession. He had thought out this move carefully, doing his best to save as much as he could of both money and freedom. But the emotional side of his character, or the spiritual side if you like, was just as strong as his reason.

*Some of the suspended officers told newspaper reporters they were innocent of wrongdoing or that they didn't know what the suspensions were all about. Most simply refused to make any comment at all. One officer was more vocal. He indignantly denied any involvement in police graft. He said his vigorous attempts to stamp out gambling had led to nine suits for false arrest against himself, amounting to $90,000. He told reporters the gamblers had promised to drop the suits if the chief took him off the Vice Squad. He said he had taken Sergeant Clark off the Vice Squad but that Chief Gabrielson had later made him take Clark back.

Esposito, a Roman Catholic, had discovered that Clark was also a Catholic. The prosecutor had advised the sergeant to confess to him as though he were talking to a priest. And it worked.

Another strange thing about his story was fear of having his money stolen. As the bribes kept coming in and he had more and more money in his possession, he didn't know what to do with it. For a time he kept it hidden in his home. But it occurred to him his house could easily be burglarized or might catch fire. He couldn't report a loss of so much money. If he did, everyone would begin wondering how a police sergeant happened to be so rich.

So he drove the streets of Chinatown night after night, collecting thousands of dollars in bribes, packing his share into a satchel that was always with him. If he had to be away from the car for awhile, he took the satchel along, even into the police station. It made a strange picture but a convincing one if you knew both Clark and the situation in Chinatown. He had reason to be afraid. The underworld knew how he carried his money. So the burly cop was at one and the same time both the hunter and the hunted. He bossed the gamblers with iron discipline, carefully punishing those who resisted the payoff with raids and harassment, collecting his bribes with the promptness of a landlord. Yet until he hit on the idea of a safe-deposit box, he was constantly afraid some thief might rob him of all he had collected.

On February 2, 1947, *The Advertiser* carried an interview with Sergeant Clark in which he gave the gist of his confession. The story called him a noted football player who was still in excellent physical condition. He may have looked pretty good, but he was not in excellent physical condition. Both Val and I knew he had an acute heart condition and high blood pressure. From the time of his confession, he carried a prayer book in his breast pocket at all times and made every effort to live righteously as he saw it. He told us he intended to retire from the Police Department when his present sick leave expired. The reason was not the graft case but his illness.

The story was now back on page one of the newspapers. Hundreds of people gathered in front of the bank at the appointed time on February 6, 1947, to get a glimpse of the sergeant when he went to open his safe-deposit box. A lot of officials had arranged to be present also. The vault was crowded with people representing the Territory of Hawaii, City and County of Honolulu, the U.S. Bureau of Internal Revenue, the bank, and both the *Star-Bulletin* and *The Advertiser.*

Bill Clark was so nervous in front of all the cameras and officials that he couldn't get the key into his safe-deposit box. A woman employee of the bank had to come to his assistance. As the photographers moved in for close-ups, Clark finally exploded in anger and shouted, "I've had enough publicity already." A cashier of the Bureau of Internal Revenue took over the contents of the box, worked busily, and came up with a report that the box contained $128,170 in cash, $6,000 in war bonds, a $400 zircon ring, three less-expensive rings, property deeds, automobile insurance policies, half a dozen Hawaiian coins, and some pre-war Japanese paper money.

The whole amount was applied by the government against a $177,500 claim the bureau had filed against Clark for unpaid taxes. This left him as poor as when he started but at least he was still out of jail. Territorial Tax Commissioner William Borthwick told the press that many gamblers who had been nailed by the Bureau of Internal Revenue were now coming into his office to admit they had also shorted the Territory. They were paying up. This made Val and me feel that maybe our effort was of some use after all.

Then the Territorial grand jury began hearing witnesses, and ten days later indictments were returned against thirteen police officers. Meanwhile, another snag cropped up. Edward Sylva, the special prosecutor Val and I had recommended, got into some heated differences of opinion with Esposito about how the graft cases should be handled. Sylva resigned.

Next, the legislature started its own probe of the way the graft investigations were being conducted and the way the prosecution was planned. At the same time, Esposito was trying to deal directly with Governor Ingram Stainback instead of Attorney General Nils Tavares. Governor Stainback didn't take kindly to Esposito, and before long a wrangle developed.

24

How It All Turned Out

ON April 23, 1947, the curtain rose on the last act of the big police graft scandal. On that day, the first trial against a police officer charged with taking bribes opened in the court of Circuit Judge Albert M. Cristy. The officer elected to waive a jury trial and leave it to the judge to give a verdict.

One highly novel element about the trial was that the three chief witnesses were just about the least likely anyone would expect to find testifying for the prosecution. They were two gamblers and Bill Clark, the cop who admitted he had received close to half a million dollars in bribes. For the first time, the public heard Paul Au's story, the size of his play at Honolulu Rooms, his description of the burly bouncers who worked as doormen, the guards who swaggered around the tables inside with bolo knives strapped to their waists, and the vicious dogs kept outside as an extra precaution. Au told his story of payoffs to the police.

Little Snake told his story about the night he got punched by a Vice Squadsman under the command of the officer on trial, and his determination to reveal the officer's bribe-taking.* Clark himself, who was used as chief witness against this officer, admitted collecting graft totaling $136,000 over a three-year period. He even described how, during the wartime blackout, he had escorted gamblers to their homes for a fee after the games closed down for the night. He said the fare for the service was between $100 and $200 depending on whether or not the gambler had been a winner or a loser.

---

*The officer on trial vigorously denied ever taking bribes from anyone. His story of the incidents described by Sau Hong Lee contradicted the gambler's version and was supported by two other police officers present. The officer on trial said Lee was regularly paid informer's fees at various times.

The defense put up an argument that became standard during all the following trials. How, asked the defense attorney, could the prosecution have the gall to come into court bringing as chief witness a man who had taken many thousands more in graft than the police officer on trial was even accused of taking? Did it seem proper to take the word of two confessed gamblers who had long records of arrests and convictions over that of a policeman who was their traditional enemy and who had a good record? Judge Cristy apparently thought not for he acquitted the police officer.

The next trial started on May 15, 1947. The police officer on trial this time was Clarence Caminos. Once more the main witnesses were Paul Au, Little Snake, and Bill Clark. Clark told how, after word got around that he had confessed, the captain had offered him $40,000 to keep his mouth shut. However, it developed the captain had only $10,000 to pay.

This case was tried before a jury. The prosecution paraded witness after witness that Val and I had dug up: a small-time gambler who said he had seen the captain and Paul Au in the office of Honolulu Rooms while gambling was going on upstairs, a handyman at the place who said he saw the captain at Honolulu Rooms five or six times, a bouncer who said 250 to 300 men gambled at the place daily playing fan-tan, monte, and dice games.

The prosecution thought they had enough witnesses by that time. Val and I disagreed. No one can tell what a jury will do when an affable man like the captain protests on the stand that he has done no wrong. It was boiling down again to the word of a veteran police officer against that of tainted witnesses. Val and I urged the prosecuting attorneys to put the small-fry gamblers from Wahiawa on the stand. In picturesque pidgin English these men described their payoffs to the likeable captain. He denied everything.

The jury was out for a little more than five hours. They came back on the morning of May 26, 1947, with a verdict of guilty against Captain Clarence C. Caminos on seven counts of bribe-taking: $900 on August 18, 1945; $500 on August 25, 1945; $2,000 on September 2, 1945; $500 on September 9, 1945; $900 on September 16, 1945; $1,900 on January 6, 1946; and $2,100 on January 13, 1946. About two weeks after the trial, Judge Cristy sentenced Caminos to a maximum term of ten years in prison and $5,000 in fines.

In the next trial over in the court of Judge Willson C. Moore, a policeman was acquitted in three days on charges of taking bribes. In July a police lieutenant went up to bat. By this time, the defense was having a field day drawing admissions from prosecution witnesses about their nefarious activities. The jury deliberated only an hour before declaring the lieutenant not guilty. He was immediately put on trial again on another count. This time the jury was out only thirteen minutes before acquitting him. He was restored to his post on the police force and retired as captain some years later.

One more big trial followed, but it was anticlimactic. Former Chief William A. Gabrielson returned from Japan to Hawaii on September 10, 1947. Public Prosecutor Esposito went after him, and the trial was set for September 29. But before the case even got to court, the prosecution nolle prossed three of the embezzlement charges. The word was that witnesses had changed their stories. Then a special prosecutor resigned, citing "professional differences" with Esposito as the reason. When the case came to court, Esposito charged Gabrielson with having financial interests in prostitution and that such interest prompted him to neglect prosecution of the bribe incidents. In two days, Esposito called sixteen witnesses and closed his case. Defense attorney O. P. Soares then moved for dismissal of the charges on the grounds that there was an utter lack of evidence to sustain the allegations of the indictment. Judge Cristy held with Soares and the case was closed.

Gabrielson fired back at Esposito after the trial. He told a reporter, "I want you to print this. He [Esposito] muffed the graft investigation completely by letting the two main principals, Clark [the sergeant] and Au [proprietor of Honolulu Rooms], go free. Instead of going after the main ones, he went after the little fellows and the result will be, as you shall see, that they will all be found not guilty."

It was one time when Gabrielson's prophecy turned out to be accurate. In November, during the trial of another police captain on bribery charges, Defense Attorney O. P. Soares told the jury the prosecution witnesses were "unworthy of credence" because they had been granted immunity from prosecution for turning state's evidence. The captain was acquitted.

By this time, prosecution of the police graft scandal had become a shambles. Governor Ingram Stainback removed Esposito from office for "demonstrated unfitness." Mayor Wilson defended Esposito, who refused to resign. A lot of legal confusion arose about who was able to fire whom. The public lost interest in the graft scandal during the ensuing political maneuvering. Then some of the gamblers who had testified disappeared because they decided it wasn't any use. The public prosecutor who succeeded Esposito nolle prossed all counts against five police officers still under indictment and against six gamblers, none of whom had been tried.

The eleven policemen who had been suspended were reinstated. They immediately started action to recover pay they had lost under suspension. Government attorneys decided they had a good case, so the Board of Supervisors voted unanimously to pay the money, $53,632. When it was all over, what had we achieved by the whole investigation? In concrete results, a box score would go something like this:

1. Chief William A. Gabrielson forced to resign.

2. Captain Clarence C. Caminos convicted and sent to prison.

3. Sergeant William Clark discharged and $134,170 recovered from his safe-deposit box.

4. More than $500,000 in taxes collected from policemen and gamblers by the U.S. Bureau of Internal Revenue and Territorial Tax Office.

5. One agent of the Bureau of Internal Revenue discharged, tried, and convicted for receiving a bribe.

6. One gambler indicted on two charges of income tax evasion. He paid $2,500 in fines and $27,000 in delinquent taxes and penalties.

7. A number of laws passed by the legislature to remove the statute of limitation on bribery of police officers regarding gambling and prostitution.

For me there were more personal memories of how it all ended. In October of 1948, Bill Clark died suddenly at his home of a heart attack. We had known he was sick, yet I was shocked when I heard that his daughter had found him collapsed in the bathroom. In the evening of the next day, Val and I drove our former boss Joseph V. Esposito and his daughter Mary to the Nuuanu Mortuary where Clark's body lay on view. We met Captain Caminos leaving the place and looking as though he had lost a close friend.

This was not the general feeling on the police force, though. As we left much later, Clark's brother stopped me and asked, "John, can you get some old-timers to act as Bill's pallbearers?"

"Sure," I answered.

"Are you sure you can get them?" he persisted, holding my arm. "The funeral is at three o'clock. I want to be sure."

"Don't worry," I told him. "I'll get them and let you know who they are first thing in the morning. I already can name three—Val, Detective Louis Camacho, and me. All I need are three more."

I got hold of three old-timers who readily agreed to serve. Next day we laid Bill Clark to rest at Diamond Head Cemetery, a man of fine character who had been tortured and killed by his failure to live up to his public trust. He had tried in the end to set things straight with his Maker, and I for one hope he succeeded.

Under the circumstances, Captain Caminos was extremely unlucky. He fought his appeal to the U.S. Supreme Court and lost. Finally he was taken to Oahu Prison to serve a ten-year sentence. After twenty-three months, he was paroled, a broken man physically. He moved to the mainland to be near a son. On January 10, 1955, he died there.

Three weeks earlier, on Christmas morning, 1954, the man who had been the principal witness against him, Paul Au, died in Honolulu. He too was virtually a broken man after the trials. He had once been wealthy, but his confessions to Val and me cost him everything he had by the time the Bureau of Internal Revenue agents finished levying taxes and penalties. Both men were in their fifties at death.

Epilogue

JOHN JARDINE worked as a special investigator in the office of the public prosecutor until December 1968. By that time he had become a familiar figure to many because of his habit of standing silently at the corner of Hotel and Bishop streets watching passersby as if they were suspects. He wore a dark suit and a hat pulled down over his eyes. When he retired, he had been on the police force for forty-five years, a record. He had served under four sheriffs and four chiefs of police, and had watched Honolulu grow from a provincial seaport town to a large city. During his police career, he had never carried a gun nor a blackjack.

On retirement, he told *Advertiser* reporter Gene Hunter:

> Honolulu has changed and civilization has advanced since I joined the police force, but the chief elements of crime and detection don't change. Crimes are committed by human beings. They may use different instruments and different techniques from year to year, but their motives are the same as those of people who committed crimes forty-five years ago.
>
> The qualities most important for a detective trying to catch a burglar, a robber or a killer are unlimited patience and attention to detail. In a real tough murder case, the man who pays attention to every small detail and finds out the meaning behind each one of them—there's the man who will catch the murderer.

Jardine added that a good policeman should have courage, common sense, a lot of luck, and the confidence of both the underworld and the general public. Hunter wrote that Jardine was noted for his underworld contacts and that, knowing he would play fair with them, they gave him many leads which helped him to solve crimes.

The detective died less than a year after his retirement at his home, on September 21, 1969. He was sixty-seven. The *Star-Bulletin* reported, "Inspector Jardine's great talent was his ability to pursue endlessly tiny scraps of evidence that would uncover those involved in Honolulu's unsolved murders. He was relentless in tracking down killers and prided himself on working, when he found time, on forgotten unsolved slayings.

"But he also had another side, a gentle side, that caused him to often hand out quarters to surprised children he saw walking down the street. He worked out of the City Prosecutor's office so many years that veterans around the police station didn't know he was on the force."

Both newspapers listed the many well-known cases Jardine solved, some of which have formed the text of this book. The list of commendations he received as a policeman could fill the pages of another book.

Production Notes

This book was designed by Roger Eggers. Composition and paging were done on the Quadex Composing System and typesetting on the Compugraphic 8400 by the design and production staff of University of Hawaii Press.

The text typeface is Garamond No. 49 and the display typeface is Compugraphic Palatino.

Offset presswork and binding were done by Vail-Ballou Press, Inc. Text paper is Writers R Offset, basis 50.